D0810469

COMMENTARIES ON THE NEW TESTAMENT
BY CHARLES R. ERDMAN

Complete in 17 volumes. $1.00 per volume

Set of 17 volumes, boxed, $15.00

AN EXPOSITION

The Epistles of Paul to the Colossians and to Philemon

By CHARLES R. ERDMAN

Professor Emeritus of Practical Theology
Princeton Theological Seminary
Princeton, New Jersey

THE WESTMINSTER PRESS

PHILADELPHIA

PRINTED IN THE UNITED STATES OF AMERICA

To
the members and friends
of the
Adirondack Community Church
Lake Placid, New York
with whom
it has been a delight
to work and to worship
during the refreshing summers
of
many joyful years

FOREWORD

Two brief letters which have come to us across the distant centuries are strikingly contrasted but inseparably united. One sets forth the most profound of religious truths; the other relates merely to the welfare of a fugitive slave. Yet both come from the same author and both have definite messages for the present age. One embodies the very essence of the Christian faith; the other shows how belief transforms and transfigures human life. Upon all the chief problems in the spheres of morality and religion these epistles shed their penetrating light.

THE EPISTLE OF PAUL
TO THE COLOSSIANS

INTRODUCTION

I. THE CHURCH AT COLOSSÆ

Colossæ was probably the least important of the cities which were prominent in the life of Paul; yet to the church in that city he wrote an epistle containing what may be regarded as his most significant and memorable statements relative to the person and work of Christ. In this epistle are named two neighboring cities closely connected with Colossæ in religious history. These are Laodicea and Hierapolis. All three were located in the valley of the river Lycos, a tributary of the Meander. They were in the Roman province of Asia, which comprised the western portion of modern Asia Minor, or more exactly of Anatolia. They were situated about one hundred and twenty-five miles southeast of Ephesus, the famous capital of the province, and on the great highway which connected Ephesus with the markets of the East. The region was known as Phrygia from the name of the Thracian invaders; for the Phrygians had occupied the country for centuries before it was incorporated into the Roman province of Asia. The population, however, was not purely Phrygian, but included many other elements, prominent among these being large numbers of Greeks and Jews.

The character of the region was mountainous and volcanic. It was frequently devastated by earthquakes. Thermal and mineral springs abounded. Furthermore, the springs which emptied into the Lycos carried great quantities of calcareous matter, which was deposited on the mountain sides and was spread along the river valley in fantastic and striking formations. The pure white stone, hanging from the cliffs, glistened "like foaming cataracts frozen in their fall."

In spite, however, of these incrustations of lime, and the volcanic character of the country, it included districts

9

of great fertility, providing rich pasture land on which were raised great flocks of sheep. Indeed the region was famous for its products of dyed wool, for, in addition to the fine quality of its fleeces, its streams furnished valuable minerals from which were produced dyes of the richest and most brilliant colors.

These factors, together with the advantage of being located on the main trade route to the Orient, brought the three cities of the Lycos Valley to a position of wealth and influence.

This was particularly true of Laodicea. Its prosperity dates from the time of its founding by Antiochus II (261–246 B.C.). Its real eminence, however, was not attained until two centuries later. In the days of Paul it was the political capital of the district, which included some twenty-five flourishing towns. It had become the home of famous philosophers, rhetoricians, and sophists. Here Cicero had spent much time and from this place he had written a number of his noted letters. Standing at the junction of four Roman roads it was the center of trade for the region and was known for its commercial activity and its wealth. The latter is attested by the fact that when the city was destroyed by a disastrous earthquake in A.D. 60, it disdained to ask for the imperial grants usually extended in such cases, but was rebuilt at its own expense. It is easy to understand how the spirit of the proud city infected the church established there, to which in one of the letters to the seven churches of Asia this message was addressed: "Thou sayest, I am rich, and have gotten riches, and have need of nothing." The greatness of the city is still further witnessed by the extent and magnificence of the ruins which after so many centuries still exist.

Laodicea was built upon terraced hills high above the valley of the Lycos. Some six miles across the valley on the heights above the banks of the river stood Hierapolis, "the city of the sanctuary" or "the sacred city." As either name implies, it was for Phrygia the chief center of religious worship. Here multitudes of priests celebrated the passionate and debasing rites of the goddess Cybele.

Here flourished also various Greek cults which united with the traditional religion in producing a moral atmosphere which was poisonous and impure.

The city was famous not only for its shrines but for its medicinal baths, and it was crowded by throngs of visitors in search of pleasure or of health. It was indeed one of the most famous of ancient watering places, and was called "the fairest of all Asia, the city of gold." However, it holds a place in history, not because of its religious ceremonies or its commercial prosperity or its rich mineral springs, but because of the casual mention of its name in the writings of an obscure missionary whom the world has come to know as the Apostle Paul.

Some twelve miles south and east of Laodicea and Hierapolis, farther up the narrow valley of the Lycos, and on both banks of the stream, certain ruins have been discovered which now are believed to mark the site of the ancient city of Colossæ. To the south Mount Cadmus rises to the height of 8,013 feet, while to the north appear the long ridges of Mount Messogis. Thus commanding the approaches to the pass through which ran the great highway between the East and the West, the city in ancient days held a place of strategic importance and attained considerable prominence. Herodotus described it as "a great city of Phrygia," at the time when in 480 B.C. Xerxes halted his great army there on the way to invade Greece. So, too, it was called by Xenophon "a populous city prosperous and great," when Cyrus encamped there on his disastrous march against Artaxerxes in 401 B.C. However, in the days of Paul the city had declined in importance before the political and commercial supremacy of Laodicea and the social popularity of Hierapolis, and it was described by a Greek historian as "a small town in the district of which the capital was Laodicea." Nevertheless, it was destined to an immortality of fame surpassing that of its two more prosperous neighbors, and this was due to the brief letter written in the first century to a group of Christians residing in this "small town" of Colossæ.

How Christianity came to be established in these cities

of the Lycos has not been definitely recorded. There can be little doubt, however, that it was due to the influence of Paul during his long stay at Ephesus while on his Third Missionary Journey. It appears that he never had visited these cities in person. This is indicated by the fact that in writing to the Colossians he makes no reference to his having been among them, and further by his statement that he had heard of their Christian faith and love, and by his intimation that his readers had never seen his "face in the flesh."

On his Second Missionary Journey, when on his way to Troas, and on his Third Journey, when on his way to Ephesus, he seems to have followed routes which lay to the north of the Lycos Valley. However, during his sojourn of three years in Ephesus the work of evangelization was widely extended throughout the whole province of Asia. Visitors from all parts of the province were continually crowding into the great capital for purposes of trade, worship, or pleasure. Many of these met the apostle whose teachings were heralded throughout the whole city. Many of these visitors accepted Christ and returned to their distant homes as joyful bearers of the "good news." Then, too, Paul was sending into the surrounding regions his chosen messengers. So wide was the movement that, according to Luke, "All they that dwelt in Asia heard the word of the Lord, both Jews and Greeks." Thus from Colossæ came Epaphras, Philemon, Apphia, and Archippus, and from Laodicea came Nymphas, all of whom received the gospel from the lips of Paul and returned to their homes to aid in the establishment of Christian churches. Others, like John Mark, may have been sent out as evangelists to work in specific places as delegates of the apostle.

To Epaphras, however, seems to be due the real honor of founding the Colossian church. He had met Paul in Ephesus and, after accepting the truth of the gospel, he seems to have been dispatched by Paul as his special messenger to Colossæ and to the other cities of the Lycos Valley. This Epaphras is probably not to be identified with Epaphroditus, the Philippian, although like him he furnished the occasion for the composition of an inspired epistle. Epaphroditus was a resident of Philippi; Epaphras was evidently a citizen of Colossæ. His labors extended, however, to Laodicea and Hierapolis and the churches of those cities were probably established by his efforts. They were certainly much upon his heart and he was continually remembering them in prayer.

The members of the Colossian church were probably Gentile converts, although not exclusively so. There were in the Lycos Valley large communities of Jews. This had been true for centuries. Some two hundred years earlier Antiochus the Great had transplanted thousands of Jews from Babylonia into Phrygia and Lydia and the colonies thus established had been enlarged by the immigration of Jewish traders. Thus there can be little doubt that among the converts to Christianity in Colossæ there were many Jews. References in the epistle written to the church indicate at least that the readers were quite familiar with Jewish customs and beliefs.

This church must have been large and influential. At first its members may have met for worship in the home of Philemon, the wealthy householder who had become acquainted with Paul in Ephesus and who, with the prayerful Epaphras, evidently had been prominent in the formation of the Colossian church. Because many of their number had been personally associated with Paul and were under the direct influence of his representative, Epaphras, the Christians in Colossæ had a clear and intelligent understanding of the great truths of the gospel. To these truths they were peculiarly loyal. In spite of the fact that they had been tempted by false teachers and had been under Jewish influences, they had remained faithful to the teachings of the apostle and were consistent in their Christian lives. The church of Colossæ, however, attained no prominence in history. While the churches of Laodicea and Hierapolis reached a position of prime importance in the early Christian centuries, the church at Colossæ soon faded from view. Nevertheless, this church transmitted to countless generations of believers a letter addressed to it by the Apostle Paul and now regarded as one of the most precious treasures of the Christian world.

II. THE COLOSSIAN HERESY

Paul always wrote with a specific purpose. Every epistle was composed to meet certain conditions and to achieve definite results. His letter to the Colossians was composed to correct certain errors of teaching which were threatening the faith of believers. Some six years had elapsed since the founding of the church. After his three years of active service in Ephesus, Paul had spent a winter in Greece and had then returned to Jerusalem, bringing rich contributions to relieve the necessity of the impoverished Christians who were members of the mother church. After a short stay in the city he had been arrested and later was confined in Cæsarea. After his appeal to Cæsar he had been conveyed to Rome where he was now awaiting his trial. In spite of the fact that he was closely guarded and was chained day and night to the arm of some Roman soldier, he was allowed a considerable degree of liberty; at least he was permitted to receive large numbers of friends and other visitors. Messengers came to him from many of the churches he had founded. In accordance with their reports Paul sent letters of instruction and encouragement to the Christian believers. Thus probably near the end of his imprisonment in Rome, possibly in the year A.D. 63, Epaphras arrived from distant Colossæ. He bore a favorable and encouraging report from the Colossian church. However, he informed Paul of certain false doctrines and practices which were endangering the beliefs and the lives of the Colossian Christians. These seemed to be of such significance that Paul composed an epistle to warn the Colossians against the threatening errors and to encourage them to live lives consistent with their Christian beliefs.

Some elements of the false teaching are easily discerned. First of all it was ritualistic. Emphasis was being laid upon the observance of sacred days and seasons and upon obedience to religious regulations and forms.

In the second place it was ascetic. In order to secure a

higher spiritual state bodily austerities were to be inflicted and natural appetites denied. Severe regulations as to food and drink were imposed.

In the third place it was mystic. There was a claim of visions and revelations, communicated only to the initiated, which were accompanied by the worship of angelic beings. Thus this false mysticism was esoteric and led to the formation of an intellectual or spiritual aristocracy.

The exact origin and classification of these errors in belief and practice are difficult to determine. Beyond all question, however, they were Jewish, either wholly or in large part. This is very evident from the emphasis laid upon the observance of feast days, of new moons, and of Sabbaths, and, further, upon the familiar rites of Judaism and its peculiar regard for the Mosaic Law. It is evident, however, that the form of Jewish doctrine which was troubling the church differed in some respects from that to which Paul refers in his Epistle to the Galatians or to the Philippians. The latter might be characterized as Pharisaic Judaism. It had in it no elements of asceticism, of mysticism, or of angel worship.

Because of these features the Colossian heresy has been regarded by some as an endeavor to unite Christian truths with the doctrine of the Essenes. It will be remembered that the Essenes with the Pharisees and the Sadducees formed the three great sects of Judaism, and many have supposed that their teachings and practices were being introduced in the Colossian church. It should be emphasized, however, that the home of the Essenes was on the west shore of the Dead Sea and we have no knowledge of their existence outside of Palestine. It is true that to a strict observance of the Mosaic Law the Essenes added a rigid asceticism. They were fond of mystic speculation and did hold an esoteric doctrine of angels, all of which appear as features of the Colossian heresy. On the other hand, the Essenes did not regard asceticism as a means to an end. They abstained from marriage, denied the resurrection of the body, forbade sacrifice, practiced communism, and were inclined to sun worship. Thus the essential elements of Essenism were absent from the false

teaching which had appeared in Colossæ, and many
scholars now regard as purely imaginary any connection
between Essene Judaism and the Colossian errors. It is,
therefore, unwise to attempt to find in Essenism the origin
of those features of the Colossian heresy which differ from
the teachings of the Judaizers mentioned in the other
epistles of Paul.

A still more popular solution of the problem regards the
Colossian heresy as Gnostic in its character. Those who
hold this view do not question that it was at the same
time Jewish. They characterize it either as Gnostic Judaism or as Jewish Gnosticism, according to the emphasis
which they lay upon the two elements which they discover
in the false teaching.

The name "Gnosticism" is commonly applied to those
forms of belief which attempted to combine Oriental theosophy and Greek philosophy with Christian doctrines.
As it appeared in its mature stage, the essential errors of
Gnosticism were found in its teachings relative to the
nature of matter and to the origin of the world. It held
that matter was in itself evil. The world, therefore, could
not have been created by God. Its origin was traced to
a series of emanations which proceeded from the divine
Being. In each successive emanation the divine element
was less prominent. The emanations were removed farther and farther from God until at last one appeared, the
Demiurge, which was of such a character that it could
create the physical universe. Somewhere between God
and man was Christ, who was himself one of these æons
or emanations. This view of matter as being in itself evil
led not only to this false conception of the person of Christ,
but was attended by practical errors. On the one hand
it led to a rigid asceticism which abused the body as being
in itself sinful; on the other hand it led to the wildest
license.

Even those who describe the Colossian heresy as being
Gnostic Judaism freely admit that true Gnosticism did
not appear earlier than the second Christian century.
However, they designate the Colossian errors as "incipient
Gnosticism." Great stress is laid upon the words "knowl-

edge" (Greek, γνῶσις) and "philosophy" (φιλοσοφία) and "fulness" (πλήρωμα) in the epistle, which are said to indicate Gnostic beliefs and to have been used by the apostle to oppose such beliefs. However, many modern scholars insist that no Gnostic implications should be attached to these words and that no trace of Gnosticism can be discovered in the entire epistle.

If the Colossian heresy, including the "worshipping of the angels," is not wholly Jewish, any other elements which it contains can probably be ascribed to the Oriental speculation, to the false mysticism, and to the mystery religions of Phrygia. It seems that the problems suggested by the errors reported to Paul as prevalent at Colossæ have been somewhat exaggerated and have been enveloped in a mist of needless speculation. Three fourths of the epistle, at least, contains little if any intimation of any peculiar philosophic or religious views, and the essential nature of the errors to which reference is made in portions of the first two chapters can in most instances be explained in the light of those Jewish influences with which all readers of the New Testament are perfectly familiar.

From any point of view it must be admitted that it is possible to identify the Colossian heresy with no exact system of teaching which existed in the days of Paul. At the same time, the rise of Gnosticism in the subsequent centuries from no definite origin or particular school of thought, but uniting in itself Christian and Jewish and Oriental elements, enables us to understand how easy it would be for errors of a somewhat similar character to make their appearance in Phrygia in the age of the apostle, and how easily speculative vagaries combined with Jewish legalism might endanger the pure doctrines of the gospel of Christ.

Two facts, however, are evident and both should be emphasized. The first is that the Colossian heresy was Christian. By this is meant that it embodied errors which were becoming prevalent in the Church. It did not indicate a schism in the Church, nor an apostasy from the Church, nor yet a distinct system of belief which was opposing the Church. It was an attempt to combine

Christian teaching with other forms of belief. In yet another sense, however, it was a Christian heresy, for the most serious phase of the problem was this: The false teaching failed to give its rightful place to the work of Christ and it failed likewise to ascribe divine and unique glory to the person of Christ.

The second vital consideration is found in the fact that every feature of this ancient heresy appears in the modern world and at this very day is endangering the purity of Christian truth and the strength of the Christian Church. Ritualism in its various forms is to be found in every part of the world. Asceticism is not widely practiced, yet its essential principle, which makes religion to consist of rules and restraints rather than a spirit of faith and of gratitude, is everywhere to be discovered. The third element of the Colossian heresy, mysticism, seems to be having a recrudescence in the modern era, when various forms of theosophy and of esoteric teaching are invading the Christian Church, when many professed followers of Christ claim to possess knowledge which is not shared by their fellow believers and attempt to form of themselves an aristocracy of faith or of knowledge or of spiritual attainment. The epistle which Paul wrote to meet these forms of error is worthy of careful study, for it shows how much that is regarded as new and advanced in thought and in doctrine is merely some form of the old heresy which was met and defeated by Paul in the first century of the Christian era.

III. THE MESSAGE OF THE EPISTLE

The best way to meet error is to emphasize truth. Negations are of little value. Controversy wins few converts. Thus when Paul has learned from Epaphras of the heresy which threatens the Colossian church, and as he writes to warn and encourage the Christian believers, he wastes no time in denouncing the false teachers or in expounding the false doctrines. In fact, he refers to the heresy in such general terms and says so little of its specific features that its exact origin and character are still subjects of conjecture and debate. However, he plainly implies that its vital fault lay in its failure to do justice to the divine person and the atoning work of Christ. Paul, therefore, sets forth, as the great burden of his message, the nature and mission of the Son of God, his place in the universe, his relation to the Church, and his complete sufficiency for all human needs.

It is this positive message which gives its real value to the epistle. It is of little importance to discover exactly what errors disturbed a church which long since has ceased to exist. What is important is the clear statement of eternal truths concerning the person and work of Christ contained in this letter which is the priceless possession of the universal Church, for these truths are the sufficient answer to the heresies which continually reappear under varying names and forms. In no place does Paul state so forcefully the fact that in Christ the whole creation finds its Source, its Supporter, and its Goal. Nowhere does he declare more impressively the limitless extent of Christ's revealing and redeeming work. Nor is the message of the epistle merely speculative. It is intensely practical. It sets forth the life which Christ makes possible for the believer, which the believer may enjoy and which the believer should reveal.

Does one yearn for a knowledge of the invisible God? He will find in Christ the image and the revelation of the Father, for in Christ dwell all the divine perfections in bodily form. Does one long for pardon and acceptance and fellowship with God? Through Christ he finds complete reconciliation with the Father. Does one aspire to an ideal moral development? This is possible by faith in Christ, by union with him, by sharing his resurrection life. These are among the great truths, needed in the present day, which are sufficient to meet and overthrow the errors that abound on every hand.

What need is there for theosophic speculation and its esoteric truths? In Christ are hidden "all the treasures of wisdom and knowledge."

Why worship saints and angels and celestial intercessors? Christ has reconciled us to God by his death. He has "delivered us out of the power of darkness" and

has "made us meet to be partakers of the inheritance of
the saints in light."

Why bear upon our consciences the burden of an elaborate ritual and observe days and fasts and ceremonies and
forms? All these are mere shadows. The substance is in
Christ.

Why attempt to attain holiness by abusing the body or
denying its innocent demands? Asceticism has no power
to curb evil desire. Holiness is attained only by setting
the heart upon Christ and by accepting the virtues which
he imparts. Christ is sufficient for all our needs. "More
than all" in him we find.

The substance of the message, therefore, may be summarized in its statement of the divine supremacy and sufficiency of Christ. He is represented as the Head of his
Body, the Church. By vital union with him believers are
spiritually "complete" and should be through with sins
and shadows, with worldly wisdom and creature worship,
and with false systems of philosophy and faith. Therefore
in all the spheres and relations of life Christians must
manifest virtues becoming those who are one with their
risen and ascended Lord.

IV. THE CONTENTS OF THE EPISTLE

The order of thought presented by the apostle as he sets
forth his notable message may be traced and analyzed as
follows:

1. The first section of the epistle may be regarded as
introductory. Col. 1:1–14. As is usual in the letters of
Paul, it contains a salutation, a thanksgiving, and a prayer.

In the salutation, Paul, a divinely appointed messenger
of Christ together with his friend Timothy, sends greeting
to the Christian brethren at Colossæ, and invokes upon
them blessing from God the Father. Vs. 1, 2.

He gives thanks for the good report he has heard of
their faith and love, animated by the heavenly hope which
was made known to them in the gospel message. He is
thankful that this true gospel which has reached them is
bearing fruit and growing at Colossæ as it is everywhere.

The immediate occasion of his thanksgiving is the visit of
Epaphras, who brought the "good news" to Colossæ as
the representative of Paul and who now has brought to
Paul the good news of the love felt toward him in Colossæ.
Vs. 3–8.

He prays that they may be granted a full knowledge of
the will of God, which may be manifest in Christian living;
that they may be fruitful in good works, which is both the
condition and the result of a fuller knowledge of God; that
they may be divinely strengthened so as to suffer and
endure not only with patience but with joy; and that they
may give thanks to God, who has qualified them "to be
partakers of the inheritance of the saints in light," who
has freed them from the tyranny of sin and translated
them into the Kingdom of his beloved Son in whom is
found redemption and divine pardon. Vs. 9–14.

2. This is an admirable introduction, for the climax of
the prayer reaches the heart of the epistle. The Son of
God and his redemption are the very themes on which
Paul is to write. He therefore proceeds at once to a doctrinal statement in which he sets forth in matchless phrases
the preëminence of Christ in his divine person and his
redeeming work.

In his relation to the Father he is declared to be the
perfect "image," or visible representation, "of the invisible God." In relation to the universe he is before and
superior to every created being or thing. In him and
through him as the divine Agent everything, visible or
invisible, has come into being. He is the Reason and Goal
of all, and the Bond of all things by whom the universe is
held together. Vs. 15–17.

Such, too, is his relation to the spiritual creation. He
is the "head" of the Church, which is his Body. He is its
Origin, its "beginning." He is the "firstborn" in the
family of those who have risen from the dead. Christ is,
therefore, supreme in both the natural and the spiritual
relation. V. 18.

The ground or reason for this supremacy is found in the
will of the Father that in the Son all the fullness of deity

should permanently abide. The purpose of this divine fullness was that by him the universe should be reconciled to God. The means of this reconciliation was the offering of his life upon the cross. The extent of this reconciliation was to include all beings "upon the earth" or "in the heavens," whether men or angels. Vs. 19, 20.

In this blessing the Colossians have their share. In their former state their hearts were hostile to God, as their conduct showed. Now by the death of Christ they have been brought into peace with God, the divine purpose being that they may be presented perfect before God. But there is one condition: They must adhere without faltering to that faith they have found, to the hope of the gospel which has been universally preached and of which Paul has been made an apostle. Vs. 21–23.

3. Of his service as an apostle Paul now proceeds to speak. It is a service which involves sufferings, yet in these he rejoices for they supplement the sufferings of Christ himself, being endured in the interests of the Church, the spiritual Body of Christ. His service is that of a stewardship intrusted by God. It consists in proclaiming the mystery once concealed but now revealed, namely, that Christ is the hope not only of one nation but of all. This Christ Paul preaches, warning and teaching every man with a view to his spiritual perfection, laboring with a strength which Christ himself imparts. Vs. 24–29.

This labor is attended by a deep solicitude, not only for the Christians at Colossæ, but for the neighboring churches and for all who have not seen Paul personally. He is concerned that they may be confirmed in faith, united in love, strengthened in their conviction, and granted a full knowledge of Christ, who is the true "mystery of God," for in him "are all the treasures of wisdom and knowledge hidden." Upon this truth Paul lays emphasis because of the danger to which the Colossians have been exposed of being led astray by plausible error. He knows that there is need to warn them of this, for, though absent from them in the body, he is so one with them in spirit that he rejoices in the orderly array and solid front which their steadfast faith in Christ presents to the foe. This attitude must be maintained. They must continue to relate themselves to Christ and to regard him as they did when first they received him. They must live in daily union with him, "rooted and builded up in him," established in their faith and "abounding in thanksgiving." Ch. 2:1–7.

4. Against the threatening peril of erroneous doctrine Paul proceeds to safeguard his readers. With this in view he contrasts the false philosophy which is being taught with the true faith that they have received. He shows the sufficiency which believers have in Christ, and then adds a twofold warning and a twofold exhortation.

The philosophy referred to was vain and misleading. It was based on human tradition. It was identified with a system of elementary religious discipline. It led its adherents away from Christ. In reality "all the fulness of the Godhead" dwells in Christ. He is the Head of all spiritual beings and every believer is complete in him.

For the Christian there is no need of adopting Jewish rites. Instead of that which is typical and physical and ceremonial, the believer has an actual experience of death to sin and resurrection to a new life of righteousness. These risen ones have been pardoned. All their sins have been forgiven. The sentence of condemnation involved in the law of ordinances has been canceled; Christ has taken it away; indeed, he has destroyed it, "nailing it to the cross." By that cross he has triumphed over all opposing powers. Vs. 8–15.

Therefore, Christians should not allow themselves to be taken to task for any failure to observe Jewish regulations as to food or fasts or festivals, which are mere shadows of the real substance found in Christ. Nor should they permit any man to rob them of their immortal prize by teaching an affected humility and the worship of angels. Such teachers did exist. They made a boast of alleged visions and were puffed up with excessive pride. As a result they lost their grasp on Christ, the Head of the Body, from

whom alone nourishment and unity and growth should be
secured.   Vs. 16–19.

On the contrary, Christians should apply to their lives
the two great spiritual principles of their death with Christ
and their resurrection with Christ. If they have died with
Christ, that should mean for them an end of the ascetic
restrictions which the false teachers are seeking to impose.
These are childish, worldly, trivial, of human origin, and
have no value in restraining the indulgence of the flesh.
Vs. 20–23.

If believers have risen with Christ they should meet
their temptations by fixing their aims and their thoughts
upon the things of the higher spiritual realm where Christ
is supreme. As by faith they share his death, so by faith
they share his life, hidden with him in God. In fact he is
their life, and when he shall again be manifested, they will
be manifested with him in glory. Ch. 3:1–4.

5. The so-called "practical" portion of the epistle, chs.
3:5 to 4:6, consists of exhortations to a manner of life
worthy of those who have died and have risen with Christ.
As members of the Christian Church, ch. 3:5–17, having
died with Christ, they must put to death "the former
habits" of impurity and unholy passion; they must put
away the old sins of temper and speech in view of the fact
that they have a new nature which is being continually
developed, and the further fact that they are living in a
new state in which artificial distinctions have vanished in
a common brotherhood. Vs. 5–11.

Since they have risen with Christ, they must cultivate
the virtues of the new life. They must "put on" compassion, sympathy, forgiveness, and love. They must let "the
peace of Christ" rule in their hearts. They must let "the
word of Christ" dwell in them richly and find its edifying
expression in sacred song. They must do everything "in
the name" of Christ, "giving thanks to . . . the Father
through him." Vs. 12–17.

In the Christian household wives and husbands must
live in the mutual relation of submission and loving devotion.   Children must be obedient to their parents, and

parents must be neither irritating nor discouraging to their children. Servants must be loyal and sincere, diligent and faithful, remembering that their real Master is the Lord, from whom they will receive their ultimate retribution or reward. So masters must be just and equitable, knowing that they "have a Master in heaven." Chs. 3:18 to 4:1.

The concluding exhortations are to perseverance in prayer, particularly in behalf of the apostle and his companions, and to discretion in deed and word, especially toward those who are outside the Christian Church. Ch. 4:2–6.

6. The personal section of the epistle presents a fascinating group of the companions of Paul. First he commends to his readers Tychicus and Onesimus, the messengers who are to convey the letter to Colossæ and are to take a full report of the circumstances and state of the apostle. Vs. 7–9.

Next he sends greetings from three Jewish Christian friends, Aristarchus, Mark, and Justus, and from three Gentile Christian friends, Epaphras, Luke, and Demas. Vs. 10–14.

He then adds greetings to his friends in Laodicea, and particularly to Nymphas. He gives instruction as to the public reading of this epistle and of a companion letter written to the Laodiceans. Lastly he sends a friendly warning to Archippus. Vs. 15–17.

7. The letter closes with a farewell salutation written by Paul's own hand. It contains a plea that his readers may remember his bonds of imprisonment and a prayer that God may grant them his grace. V. 18.

THE OUTLINE

I. The Preface.   Col. 1:1–14

1. the salutation.   Ch. 1:1, 2

1 Paul, an apostle of Christ Jesus through the will of God, and Timothy our brother, 2 to the saints and faithful brethren in Christ *that are* at Colossæ: Grace to you and peace from God our Father.

The salutation which opens the Epistle to the Colossians follows the form familiar in letters of the day. Its Christian notes, however, give to it a distinctive dignity and majesty. These mark it as belonging to that group of inspired writings which were destined to be the priceless possession of every age and land.

As was usual in such a salutation, it contains the name of the writer and of his readers, and an expression of his concern for their highest welfare. In mentioning his name Paul also calls himself "an apostle of Christ Jesus"; he describes his readers as "saints and faithful brethren in Christ"; and the benefits he invokes are "from God our Father."

Paul's is a name which at once arrests the attention and fires the imagination. The figure of the great apostle towers above that of all others in the latter half of the first Christian century. His personality presents the unusual combination of a keen intellect, a tender heart, and an indomitable will. He also was a Roman citizen by birth and possessed the combined culture of the Greek and the Jew. These qualities and advantages prepared him for his notable career. Within a few years he planted Christian churches in the chief centers of the Roman Empire, and largely determined the course of future history. It is with a thrill of emotion that one holds in his hand a letter which actually came from the mind and heart of this great hero.

That Paul was the author of this epistle is not to be doubted. It is true that modern theories which claimed to find in the epistle references to the Gnosticism of the second century denied this authorship, but more recent and restrained views of the false doctrines to which the writer alludes have been attended by a new and even more positive assertion that here is an authentic production of the Apostle Paul.

He was writing from Rome. Of this there need be no doubt. It is true that some scholars have conjectured that the place was Cæsarea, and others that it was Ephesus; but these theories are far from being established. It seems that Paul had completed his three historic missionary journeys, had been arrested in Jerusalem, had been conveyed to Cæsarea, and had been transferred to the Imperial City. Here, while awaiting his trial and while under military guard, he found frequent opportunities for preaching, he received friends from the city and representatives from distant lands, and he carried on a wide correspondence with the churches which he had founded.

Among the letters written during this period, four are found in the New Testament. These are the Epistles to the Philippians, to the Ephesians, to the Colossians, and to Philemon. The three last named are closely related. All were to be sent to the province of Asia. Two were to be sent by the same messenger, Tychicus, who was to be accompanied by Onesimus as he carried his letter to Philemon, whose home was in Colossæ. The two intrusted to Tychicus, namely Ephesians and Colossians, are companion epistles. The main theme of the first is the Church, of which Christ is the Head. The main theme of the second is Christ, the divine Head of his Body, the Church.

As in opening this letter to the Colossians Paul designates himself "an apostle of Christ Jesus," he employs a phrase which has in it the note of authority. He is writing to correct certain false views which have been reported to him. He therefore uses the term "apostle" in its fullest sense. He claims a perfect equality with the Twelve. He assumes what he elsewhere asserts, that he possesses all the qualifications of apostleship, namely, that he has seen the risen Christ, that he is an inspired witness to the resurrection, and that in the gift of performing miracles he has "the signs of an apostle." When he calls himself "an apostle of Christ Jesus," he means that he has been sent forth as a chosen representative of Christ, that this commission came from Christ directly and personally, and that the very sphere and substance of his apostolic service is his testimony concerning Christ.

Furthermore, he declares that his apostleship is "through the will of God." This sense of a divine vocation was always strong in the mind of Paul. He was ever conscious that he had received a divine calling. Such should be the conviction of everyone who trusts and follows Christ. He should be inspired by the belief that his life and his tasks are ordered by God, and that, in whatever sphere he may be placed, his career may be regarded as an exalted and a lofty destiny.

With his own name Paul unites that of Timothy. He does not intend to add authority by the mention of this name. It is rather an act of courtesy, for Timothy was his voluntary companion in imprisonment. During the long years of travel and of toil, since the beginning of his First Missionary Journey, Timothy had been Paul's most trusted comrade. This young friend of the apostle was a man of unselfish sympathy and unstinted devotion. He was delicate, frequently ill, naturally timid, hesitant, in need of encouragement, affectionate even to "tears"; yet in no one else did Paul repose greater confidence, on no other did he lavish such love. He was Paul's most loyal follower and imitator, his fellow worker, his "true child in faith." Timothy may have never visited the Colossians, but he was known to them, and the mention of his name in the salutation was, on the part of Paul, a delicate recognition of his presence and an appreciation of his companionship.

Paul describes him only as "Timothy our brother." Timothy was not an apostle, and Paul gives him the simplest possible designation as a Christian. Yet it is significant. It recognizes that fellowship of believers which constitutes the most perfect brotherhood the world has ever known. Because of their common faith in Christ, Timothy was a "brother," not only to Paul, but also to those readers whom he may never have seen.

Those readers are described as "saints and faithful brethren in Christ." In the time of Paul the term "saints" was applied to all believers. It did not denote a special group which possessed eminent virtues, nor did it refer to such as had passed from earth to heaven. All who trusted in Christ were "saints." The word originally indicated separation, and specifically separation unto God. Then it came to indicate the moral purity which results from such separation. While used by Paul as the common description of all church members, still the word embodied a certain ideal. In reality all Christians do belong to God, and upon them all rests the obligation to manifest such holiness as this relationship implies. "Saints" is a name of dignity and honor, and also of hope. Those to whom it has been given should expect to become in character and experience what they already are in the mind and purpose of God.

These saints are further described as "faithful brethren in Christ." They are "faithful" in the sense not only of being trustworthy but also of being trustful. They are "believers." It is their faith which has brought them into their relation to God, and also into their relation to one another. The former relation is that of "saints." The latter relation is that of "brethren." The last word is a beautiful designation of that surprising new fellowship which the church constituted. It was composed of masters and slaves, of rich and poor, of Greeks and barbarians, of Gentiles and Jews; yet all these members recognized themselves as forming an actual brotherhood, a household of faith.

This faith was "in Christ." The phrase is used by Paul to express the deepest truth, the most profound reality, in the whole sphere of his belief and teaching. By it he meant to define that mystical union which exists between Christ and the believer, that relation by which Christ becomes the very sphere in which one lives. His purposes, his hopes, his endeavors are all "in Christ"; indeed, for him "to live is Christ." Here, however, the phrase need not be pressed to its full meaning. It may be used merely in the sense of "Christian." Possibly it may only define the "brethren" as "Christian brethren." More probably it refers to the whole phrase and describes "the saints and faithful brethren" as "Christian." In any case, it gives a dignity to the readers whom Paul addresses and intimates something of the large significance which is attached to the terms by which the members of the Early Church were called. They were "disciples," for they were learning of Christ. They were "saints," for they belonged to God. They were "brethren," for they were in one spiritual brotherhood. They were "believers," for they shared one common faith. They were "Christians," for they found in Christ the sum and substance of their lives. There are messages here for all who bear these names. They are "disciples": they must seek fuller knowledge. They are "saints": they must be pure. They are "brethren": they must show their love. They are "believers": they must "live by faith." They are "Christians": they must center their lives in Christ.

Those whom Paul describes by such significant if familiar names were "at Colossæ." In his day the place was of no great importance. Situated in Phrygia, southeast of Ephesus, in the valley of the Lycos, it became increasingly obscure, and sank in forgotten ruins. However, this single mention of its name by Paul has made the city actually immortal in the memory of men.

How it came to pass that Christians were residing there is nowhere explained. From references which follow in this epistle it would appear that the city never had been visited by Paul. However, during his long stay in Ephesus, a convert to Christianity, Epaphras by name, seems to have brought to the city the glad tidings of the gospel. Now that Paul was a prisoner in Rome this same Epaphras brought him a report to the effect that while this gospel was still making progress in Colossæ, it was in danger of being corrupted by false teachings. These doctrines seemed to combine Jewish ritualism and Oriental mysticism. To warn his readers against such errors, and to

present the supremacy and preëminence of Christ, Paul
sent them the epistle which follows.

Paul concludes his salutation, however, by expressing
to his readers this ardent desire: "Grace to you and peace
from God our Father." Thus, with a slight change in
form, Paul unites the greetings familiar in the Western
and the Eastern worlds. In Greek correspondence the
usual greeting was χαίρειν, translated "rejoice," "hail,"
"salute." Paul substitutes χάρις, translated "grace," a
word from the same root but with a quite different meaning. It denotes favor, and frequently favor toward the un-
deserving. When united with the phrase "from God our
Father," it indicates the love of God which makes him
willing to pardon and to bless. Then, too, it indicates the
gifts which such love bestows, and still further the effects
of these gifts in the ennobling of conduct and the beauti-
fying of character.

To this greeting, thus related to the Greek salutation,
Paul adds the customary greeting of the Hebrew, namely,
"Peace." This likewise is immeasurably enriched by being
related to "God our Father" as its source. It includes
peace with God, peace with men, and most of all that
peace from God, that quietness and tranquillity of soul,
which can protect from all anxiety and wrong and can
guard the heart and the thoughts in Christ Jesus. These
bestowals of "grace" and "peace," rightfully belong to
all who by faith are members of the brotherhood of Christians and rejoice in the fatherhood of God.

Such then is the salutation of Paul to the Colossians;
and thus the Spirit of Christ can change a formal greeting
into a psalm, a sermon, a treasury of truth.

2. THE THANKSGIVING. Ch. 1:3–8

3 We give thanks to God the Father of our Lord Jesus
Christ, praying always for you, 4 having heard of your faith
in Christ Jesus, and of the love which ye have toward all the
saints, 5 because of the hope which is laid up for you in the
heavens, whereof ye heard before in the word of the truth
of the gospel, 6 which is come unto you; even as it is also in

all the world bearing fruit and increasing, as *it doth* in you also, since the day ye heard and knew the grace of God in truth; 7 even as ye learned of Epaphras our beloved fellow-servant, who is a faithful minister of Christ on our behalf, 8 who also declared unto us your love in the Spirit.

Words of appreciation may prepare the heart to accept warning and advice. Thus, as in most of his epistles, Paul follows his greeting to the Colossians by a thanksgiving for the virtues they possess and for the progress they are making in the Christian life. His praise is sincere, his purpose is honest; yet such an approach to his readers reveals Paul's natural courtesy and also his tact and wisdom in dealing with his fellow beings.

However, a still more important principle is involved. Thanksgiving should always precede intercession. In all worship, private and public, gratitude should be expressed before petitions are offered. Paul is about to state the requests which he is continually making in his prayers for the Colossians. He very properly mentions first the praise to God which forms so large a part in those prayers.

Furthermore, this habit of turning to God with thanksgiving explains in large measure Paul's hopeful attitude toward the churches he addresses, and the boldness of his requests for their spiritual progress. The remembrance of divine mercies in days that are past enables one to regard the future with cheer and to pray with confidence. The thanksgiving here expressed is for the faith and hope and love of the readers and for the fruit of the gospel among them. It is addressed "to God the Father of our Lord Jesus Christ." The phrase should raise no question as to the deity of "our Lord." There is a reality in his divine and unique sonship. He is the "only begotten Son," and while claiming an equality with the Father, he could speak to his followers of "my Father and your Father," of "my God and your God."

To this Father God Paul gives continual thanks for the Colossians. The various English versions raise the unimportant question whether Paul means to say that he gives thanks whenever he prays or that his thanksgiving forms a part of his continual prayer. Possibly the former is his intention here. When he turns to mention his petitions he emphasizes the ceaselessness of his prayer. Here he lays stress on his unceasing praise.

The occasion of thanksgiving is the good report brought to Paul concerning the Christians at Colossæ. The ground of the thanksgiving is their faith and love and hope. How these three terms are here related, it is rather difficult to determine. Usually they describe the familiar triad of Christian graces, and that conception could not have been absent from the mind of the writer. However, he does not treat hope, in this instance, as a grace or a virtue. It is an object toward which his readers turn in confident expectation, but strictly it is not something they feel within themselves but a reality to which they look. It is not dwelling in their hearts but is laid up for them "in the heavens."

Their "faith" is described as being "in Christ." The Greek phrase seems to indicate that Christ is regarded, not only as the object of their faith, but as the sphere in which this faith is exercised. The "faith" not only rests upon Christ; it is "in Christ." It is inspired by him and is exercised in vital union with him.

"The love" is felt and expressed "toward all the saints," that is, toward all the Christian believers. The reference is probably not to the Church universal, but to all members of the brotherhood in Colossæ, whatever their rank or station or sphere in life.

"The hope" denotes the future heavenly blessedness which awaits all believers. It centers in Christ who is himself called "our hope." It will be consummated when he appears in glory. Some students connect this word "hope" directly with the phrase, "We give thanks," as being the specific ground of Paul's gratitude for the Colossians, while his hearing of their faith and love are its occasion. Possibly it may be better to regard it as a stimulus to their faith, and as an inspiration to deeper love for those by whom this common Christian hope is to be shared.

In any case, the thanksgiving centers upon this hope, more than upon faith and love. Paul declares to his readers

not only that it "is laid up for you in the heavens," but
that it forms an essential and prominent element in the
gospel message; for he adds, in reference to this hope,
"Whereof ye heard before in the word of the truth of the
gospel." This was for the Colossians no novel message.
They had heard it "before," that is, in the earlier days
of their Christian experience. This heavenly hope had
been revealed to them by the proclamation of that revealed
truth which constituted the gospel.

Some have conjectured that Paul mentions "the truth"
to warn his readers against the false doctrine prevalent in
Colossæ. This would be a diversion of thought. The
emphasis here is not upon "the truth" as opposed to
error, but upon the gospel as conveying that element of
"the truth" for which Paul is returning thanks, namely,
"the hope" laid up in heaven.

This gospel, Paul declares, has come not only to the
Colossians but to "all the world." This must not be
regarded as a questionable exaggeration, but as a strong
figure of speech. It is true that many localities had not
been reached but it is also true that the gospel had been
preached in most of the provinces of the Roman Empire;
its progress was still rapid, and its power was manifest.
It was showing itself to be adapted to all races and conditions of men. It was "bearing fruit and increasing"; for
it was revealing not only an inherent energy but an
external growth. It was changing the conduct and the
character of those it had reached, and it was spreading
throughout the whole world.

The gospel is not a mere system of ethics; it is a trans-
forming power, even "the power of God unto salvation to
every one that believeth." It was designed not only for
those in proud political and intellectual centers but also
for all the peoples of the earth.

Paul is thankful that this gospel has been bearing its
previous fruit and extending its blessed influence among
the Colossians "since the day [they] . . . heard and knew
the grace of God in truth." "The grace of God" was the
very essence of the gospel message, as this is elsewhere
called "the gospel of the grace of God." The message of

unmerited favor, of loving forgiveness, of sustaining strength, of eternal hope, began to manifest its power among the Colossian believers from the very day when they heard and understood its divine reality. The phrase "in truth" is commonly understood as another indication that Paul is referring to the contrasted heresy being taught in Christ. It is evident that these references to the real nature and power of the gospel do form a proper preface to a letter in which false doctrine is rebuked. However, it is not necessary to insist upon detecting such subtle allusions to error in this joyous paragraph of thanksgiving and praise.

The gospel of which Paul is speaking had been brought to the Colossians by Epaphras, as here intimated: "Even as ye learned of Epaphras our beloved fellow-servant." This is not merely an indorsement of the doctrine they had received or an assurance that "they had no need to listen to strange teachers," but is rather a gracious recognition of the faithful friend who recently had brought from distant Colossæ tidings to Paul now imprisoned in Rome.

The name Epaphras is an abbreviation of Epaphroditus, but there is no reason to conclude that Epaphras is to be identified with the Epaphroditus mentioned in the Epistle of Paul to the Philippians. The latter was evidently a resident of Philippi and an active worker in the church of that Macedonian city, while Epaphras was a representative of the church in Colossæ. He seems from this passage to have been the founder of that church.

Paul designates him here as "a faithful minister of Christ on our behalf." This is taken to mean that Epaphras probably had been commissioned by Paul to bear the gospel message to Colossæ. It must have been while Paul was residing in Ephesus, during the time of his Second Missionary Journey. At that time, by such representatives of the apostle, the whole province of Asia was evangelized and churches were organized in Colossæ, in Hierapolis, and in Laodicea, as well as in other places. Epaphras is supposed by some to have been the founder of all three of these churches. In any case it appears that he was the messenger who brought to Paul the tidings of heresies threatening the infant church at Colossæ. Of such report no mention is made, although the prominent mention of Epaphras here, and the statement of the deep solicitude of Epaphras for the Colossians recorded in the last chapter, lead to the conclusion that Epaphras was the bearer of the message which led Paul to compose this epistle.

One must not attach to the word "minister" ideas which belong to its modern usage. It did not designate a pastor, a preacher, or a local church official. It meant a "servant," a "helper." Undoubtedly Epaphras did preach the gospel at Colossæ; but Paul meant that he had been serving in his place and as his representative. As a result of such faithful service the church had been founded.

Probably this same devoted servant of Christ had brought to Paul the news of the false teaching at Colossæ. This is not stated. Paul records a message more in harmony with this paragraph of thanksgiving when he says that Epaphras has "declared unto us your love in the Spirit." Years before Epaphras had brought the gospel to Colossæ as the representative of Paul; now he has brought this expression of love from the Colossians to Paul. It was not the love which springs from personal acquaintance and friendship, such as was felt for Paul by the Philippians. It was that sympathy and affection which the Holy Spirit inspires toward those who have never seen one another in the flesh but who share a common faith and hope centering upon Christ. The mention of such love forms a fitting climax to this outburst of praise with which the epistle begins.

3. THE PRAYER.   Ch. 1:9–14

9 For this cause we also, since the day we heard *it*, do not cease to pray and make request for you, that ye may be filled with the knowledge of his will in all spiritual wisdom and understanding, 10 to walk worthily of the Lord unto all pleasing, bearing fruit in every good work, and increasing in the knowledge of God; 11 strengthened with all power, according to the might of his glory, unto all patience and longsuffering with joy; 12 giving thanks unto the Father, who made us

meet to be partakers of the inheritance of the saints in light;
13 who delivered us out of the power of darkness, and translated us into the kingdom of the Son of his love; 14 in whom
we have our redemption, the forgiveness of our sins.

Paul prayed. We can find inspiration in this very fact.
Prayer, then, need not be regarded by intelligent people
as a delusion, a superstition, an impertinence, as some
would have us believe.   Prayer is a reality; it is the enjoyment of a glorious privilege, the exercise of a measureless
power.

A large portion of Paul's time was spent in this pursuit.
The "anxiety for all the churches" he had established
found its natural expression in earnest intercession in
their behalf.   In the preface of the epistle written to any
one of these churches he states the requests which formed
the substance of these daily supplications.   There were
in each case petitions appropriate to the particular need.
However, these opening prayers of the apostle indicate
exactly the requests which should be offered for the
churches of the present day, and indeed for each individual
Christian.   They form possibly the most precious portions of the New Testament epistles.

In the case of the letter to the Colossians the chief petition is for spiritual knowledge.   This may be regarded as
specially pertinent to the situation of the church.   It was
being disturbed by false teachers who were making great
boasts of possessing superior wisdom and of sharing secret
mysteries and revelations.   No wonder that Paul here
prays for true knowledge.   Yet it should be noted that
this same request is prominent in his prayers for other
churches, and that it should be offered quite as truly for
the churches of to-day.   Furthermore, the knowledge for
which Paul prayed was not merely speculative but such
as would manifest itself in right conduct, in service, and
in thanksgiving to God.

"For this cause," writes the apostle, referring to the
good report he has received from Epaphras as to the
faith and love and spiritual progress of his readers, "we
also," that is, in response to this report, "do not cease to

pray and make request for you." This is not an exaggeration. Paul does not mean that the utterance of his requests was continual, but that at no time has he ceased from the habit of praying for this church. "That ye may be filled with the knowledge of his will," is the burden of Paul's prayer. By "his will" he means, of course, "the will of God." It is not a request to know the nature of God, which might result in mere intellectual gratification, but to know the will of God as to right conduct, which should issue in moral resolution.

This "knowledge of his will" results in "all spiritual wisdom and understanding." For this also Paul prays. "Wisdom" is the larger and more general term. It is the highest form of knowledge. It indicates here the apprehension of moral principles, while "understanding" implies the ability to apply such principles to particular problems. This wisdom and discernment are defined as "spiritual," because they have their source not in human reasoning and discovery but in God himself; they are the product of his Holy Spirit.

The divine purpose in granting such "knowledge" is that right conduct may result. So Paul requests for his readers this "spiritual wisdom and understanding" in order that they may "walk worthily of the Lord unto all pleasing." "Walk" is a figurative expression for the course of life. Paul would have these Christians live worthy of their profession, worthy of the Lord who had given them his example of moral perfection, worthy of him who had died for them, worthy of him who was ever granting them the graces of his Spirit. Their manner of conduct should ever be such as to win his approval and to merit his praise. It should be "unto all pleasing."

So Paul ever united doctrine and duty, knowing and doing. Right action will result from right thinking, and right thinking will accompany right conduct. Thus the life which results from true knowledge will be a life "bearing fruit in every good work, and increasing in the knowledge of God." There are those who prefer to render this phrase, "Bearing fruit and increasing in every good work by the knowledge of God." The reason for this preference is that Paul has already recorded his petition for an increase "in the knowledge of God," and that probably he is expressing here his desire for a life of increasing fruitfulness and goodness produced "by the knowledge of God."

The ideas are vitally related to each other and to the petition for spiritual strength which follows. Indeed, this strength may be regarded as issuing from this knowledge, or as characterizing the life in which the knowledge results. In his other letters also Paul unites requests for knowledge with requests for spiritual power. Here his petition is that the Colossians may be "strengthened with all power, according to the might of his glory." This strength will be that of character, of conviction, and of moral action. It will be in response to, and will be proportioned to, the "might of his glory." God's glory is his manifested excellence. Here it is the greatness of his revealed might. The supply of spiritual strength, therefore, upon which the Christian may depend is measured by the limitless power which God has manifested in and toward men.

How is this power to be employed? Not in the working of miracles, not in outbursts of eloquence, not in spectacular martyrdoms, but in producing the homely virtues of "patience and longsuffering." "Patience" implies steadfast endurance in the face of opposition, of temptation, and of trials; "longsuffering" denotes the forbearance that in the face of insult or injury does not seek to retaliate or to take revenge.

To "patience and longsuffering" Paul adds the phrase, "With joy." It is possible to endure and to forbear with a spirit which is stoical and sour; but it should be possible for a Christian to meet difficulties and to endure wrongs with a temper of buoyant and triumphant gladness. This, indeed, will require the strength which God alone can give.

Last of all, Paul mentions thanksgiving as the crowning result of the spiritual knowledge for which he prays, or as a third characteristic of the life in which a true knowledge of the will of God will issue. It will be a life of service, a life of strength, but also a life of praise. "Giving thanks unto the Father," writes Paul. The very designation of God by the name "Father" might well awaken a spirit of gratitude. It points to the loving Source from which comes "every good gift and every perfect gift." However, Paul specifies the definite and divine bestowals which constitute the grounds of Christian gratitude. These grounds center in the realities of light and love and liberty.

"Who made us meet to be partakers of the inheritance of the saints in light" is stated as the first reason for thanksgiving. To be made "meet" does not mean to be made worthy, but to be made competent, to be given the title. It does not denote character, but privilege, or position, or right. "Saints" indicates Christians, all true Christians. To them belongs a glorious heritage in the Kingdom of light. They are already qualified for its possession. Some of its blessedness they now enjoy, but its full fruition is one with "the hope which is laid up . . . in the heavens" for which Paul returns thanks as the letter opens.

He next shows how this right has been secured. It has been obtained by the goodness of God, "who delivered us out of the power of darkness, and translated us into the kingdom of the Son of his love." Here "darkness" and "light" are strongly contrasted. When a man accepts Christ as his Saviour he is set free from the powers of evil and becomes a citizen of the realm of light in which Christ reigns. This Kingdom is also a realm of love, for the Son who rules is the supreme object of the Father's affection. He is the well-beloved Son; he is "the Son of his love."

In fellowship with this Son, and by faith in him, we have deliverance and pardon; for he it is "in whom we have our redemption, the forgiveness of our sins." Christians are thus compared, not only to captives who have been delivered by force, but to such as have been ransomed by the payment of a price. This ransom is described elsewhere as the blood of Christ, who gave himself to set his people free. The main idea here, however, is not in the price paid, but in the freedom secured. The word "redemption" is here used to describe deliverance from the guilt and penalty of sin. This, however, is not the whole of redemption. It is the first experience of a believer, and a vitally important experience.   However, "redemption" as set forth in the New Testament will be complete only when the perfected spirit is clothed with an immortal body.

Such are the abundant reasons for thanksgiving given by Paul to the Colossian Christians.   Thus, too, by the mention of the beloved Son and his redeeming work, does he bring his readers to the specific theme and very heart of his epistle, for Paul is to write a message which is chiefly concerned with the divine person and the saving work of Christ.

II. The Preëminence of Christ.   Ch. 1:15–23

1. his divine person.   Ch. 1:15–18

15 Who is the image of the invisible God, the firstborn of all creation; 16 for in him were all things created, in the heavens and upon the earth, things visible and things invisible, whether thrones or dominions or principalities or powers; all things have been created through him, and unto him; 17 and he is before all things, and in him all things consist. 18 And he is the head of the body, the church: who is the beginning, the firstborn from the dead; that in all things he might have the preëminence.

Error is met best by the positive statement of truth. The error need not always be explained and expanded and its undisputed elements defended. All this is often confusing and even misleading. Of course it is helpful to know the main fallacies which are being corrected. However, the best defense is in the form of definite and convincing affirmation. Thus when Paul writes to combat the false teaching at Colossæ he does not make plain the exact nature of the Colossian heresy. This is still a matter of conjecture and of debate. He does make clear, however, its main defects. Evidently it involved the worship of angelic beings and the dependence upon ceremonies and forms to secure acceptance with God.

To meet these errors Paul sets forth the divine nature and the absolute sufficiency of the person and work of Christ. He does not first define the false doctrine. He begins with no clear allusion to it. Yet he states truths of such unquestioned reality and such abiding importance that they have been of priceless value in meeting every form of heresy that ever has threatened the essential beliefs of the Christian Church.

In the opening thanksgiving and prayer which form the preface to the epistle Paul already has stated these truths. Indeed it is difficult, if not impossible, to determine where the prayer ends and where the teaching begins. In his prayer he has declared Christ to be the Son of God, "the Son of his love," and has described Christ as the Redeemer and Deliverer from the realm and power of darkness and sin, the Lord of the Kingdom of light. He now opens his discussion by a fuller statement of the divine nature and saving work of Christ. In fact this forms the very theme of the letter.

As to the nature of Christ, Paul sets forth his unique majesty and supreme dignity by showing his relation to God, to the created universe, and to the Church. First of all he declares him to be "the image of the invisible God." The word "image" means a likeness, but also a representation and, further, a manifestation. It includes the three ideas of "resemblance, representation, revelation." It expresses such a likeness as that of a head stamped upon a coin, or such a representation as that of a face reflected in a mirror; yet its fuller meaning, as here, is that of an exact representation. The likeness of the Son to the Father was so perfect as to fit him to be the complete and final revelation of God to men. In this sense Christ is declared to be "the image of the invisible God."

In describing God as "invisible," Paul does not mean merely that he is not visible to physical sight, but that he cannot be discovered by the unaided reason and intellect and imagination. God cannot be known except in and through Christ. "He hath declared him." We behold "the light of the knowledge of the glory of God in the face of Jesus Christ." "He that hath seen me hath seen the Father," was the claim made by Christ himself, who also declared, "Neither doth any know the Father, save the Son, and he to whomsoever the Son willeth to reveal him."

Such a revelation as Christ gives enables man to know a God who can be trusted and obeyed and loved. Hungering human hearts are not willing to accept the verdict that there is no God; nor are they satisfied with abstractions concerning "the Absolute," "the Unknowable," or "the Reign of Law." In Christ is found a God who is near, who cares, who hears, who pities, and who saves.

Paul further shows the uniqueness and preëminence of
Christ by stating his relation to the created universe.
He declares that Christ is "the firstborn of all creation,"
that "in him" and "through him" and "unto him" were
"all things . . . created," and that "he is before all
things, and in him all things consist."   Vs. 15–17.

"The firstborn of all creation" might seem to mean
that Christ was himself part of the Creation and himself
a created Being were it not for the fact that the rest of
the paragraph deals wholly with the truth that Christ was
not created, but himself was the Creator.   Paul could
not possibly contradict himself so absolutely in one sentence.   "Firstborn" here means two things: priority in
time and supremacy in place or position.   Christ existed
before the Creation, but he held the rank commonly
assigned to the "firstborn," the rank of eminence and
dominion.   Christ is thus declared to be the universal
Sovereign.

In contrast with his being a Creature, all things were
created "in him" and "through him" and "unto him";
that is, he is the Source, the Agent, and the Goal of all
creation.   Or, expressed in more technical terms, he is
"the conditioning Cause," "the mediating Cause," "the
final Cause" of all things.

"In him" all creative force resided and was definitely
put forth; "in him" existed all the laws and activities
which became manifest in the world.   Yet he was and is
ever distinct from the world.   "Through him" were all
things.   He was the medium of divine energy, yet not as
a mere passive instrument.   He was working with the
Father, and the work was so truly his that John could
say, "All things were made through him; and without him
was not anything made that hath been made."

He, too, is the Goal of all creation, its final Cause.   He
contains in himself the reason why creation exists and
why it is what it is.   Toward him all movements con-
verge.   In his Kingdom ultimately all creatures will
realize the eternal purpose of God.

Nor is Paul satisfied with the inclusive phrase, "All

things." He insists that the supremacy of Christ is not bounded by the material universe, but includes all spiritual beings as well. Thus Paul presents the creation in two distinct, exhaustive divisions, as consisting of things "in the heavens and upon the earth, things visible and things invisible." "Invisible" things seem to be specified by the added phrase, "Whether thrones or dominions or principalities or powers."

Paul probably mentions this celestial hierarchy to meet the false teachings prevalent at Colossæ. These teachings included the worship of angels, who were exalted to a place belonging to Christ alone. There is no reason to conclude that Paul believed in the existence and gradation of these angelic beings. What he means is to insist that Christ is the Creator and Sovereign of all rulers and powers, human and superhuman; he is superior to all spirits that are reverenced, whether they are imaginary or real. Paul does not pause to inquire how much or how little of truth there is in the speculations about celestial beings. He declares emphatically that all forces, powers, and beings in the universe, of whatever character or kind, are inferior and subject to Christ.

That Christ is the Creator of all things, including not only these angelic beings but the entire universe, Paul again affirms. The statement is more brief but possibly more emphatic: "And he is before all things, and in him all things consist." Paul asserts not only that Christ was before all things, but that "he is before all things," for his existence is absolute, changeless, eternal. Furthermore, "in him all things consist"; they "hold together"; they form "a cosmos instead of a chaos." He is both the Creator and the Sustainer of the universe. He maintains its harmony, its order, its life.

This view of nature and of the whole realm of being, as created and controlled by Christ, is arresting and majestic. To see Christ as "existent behind all laws," to regard stars and atoms, and the worlds of men and of angels, as "in him" and "through him" and "unto him," is to gain a wholly new and overwhelming vision of his glory and to find a new beauty and splendor in the universe he has made and ever sustains.

Paul now mentions a third relationship in order to establish the absolute preëminence of Christ. He first has been shown to be the Image of God, secondly the Creator of the universe, now, in the third place, the Head of the Church: "And he is the head of the body, the church: who is the beginning, the firstborn from the dead." It is evident that Paul intends to contrast the material or natural creation with the spiritual or new creation. In both spheres Christ is supreme.

The figure of speech which describes the relation of Christ to his Church as that of the Head to the Body is familiar to all Christians. It is expanded in the first letter to the Corinthians, where Paul is showing the mutual relations of church members. It is prominent in the letter to the Ephesians. The difference is that in the latter epistle the emphasis is laid upon the Church, as the Body of which Christ is the Head, while in Colossians the thought is centered upon Christ, who is the Head of the Body.

The figure indicates that Christ is the Source from which the Church derives its life and power and strength; that he unites its members in one indivisible organism; and that, above all, he controls and directs the Church, of which he is the divine and living Head.

Paul further declares that this headship is due to the fact that Christ is "the beginning, the firstborn from the dead." Thus the figure of speech is somewhat changed. The Church is pictured not only as a body, of which believers are the members. It is also a family, of which Christ is the first-born. The family is composed of those who share with Christ his resurrection life. He is the "beginning." The word denotes not merely the first in a series, but also the source to which the series can be traced. The term is defined by the words which follow: "The firstborn from the dead." Christ was the first to rise from death never to die again. The fact that he is the "firstborn" implies that others follow. The fact

that he is the "beginning" indicates that their resurrection
is due to his power.

This resurrection which Christ secures is both spiritual
and physical. In this very epistle Paul declares that
believers already have been "raised together with Christ"
to a new and higher life, and yet he also implies the future
resurrection of the body when he states that "when
Christ, who is our life, shall be manifested, then shall ye
also with him be manifested in glory."

Of these followers who now share his life he is the
"firstborn." The term here again indicates not only
priority but also sovereignty. He is not only the first
to rise, but of these risen ones he is the Master and Lord.
Thus, he who is the Creator and Ruler of the universe is
likewise the Source and Sovereign of the new spiritual
creation, the Church.

This is in fulfillment of the purpose of the Father for
his Son. It is according to his divine will "that in all
things," whether in the natural or in the spiritual world,
"he might have the preëminence."

2. HIS RECONCILING WORK. Ch. 1:19–23

19 For it was the good pleasure *of the Father* that in him
should all the fulness dwell; 20 and through him to reconcile
all things unto himself, having made peace through the blood
of his cross; through him, *I say*, whether things upon the
earth, or things in the heavens. 21 And you, being in time
past alienated and enemies in your mind in your evil works,
22 yet now hath he reconciled in the body of his flesh through
death, to present you holy and without blemish and unreprovable before him: 23 if so be that ye continue in the faith,
grounded and stedfast, and not moved away from the hope
of the gospel which ye heard, which was preached in all
creation under heaven; whereof I Paul was made a minister.

Having set forth the preëminence of Christ in his being
the Image of God, the Creator of the universe, and the
Head of the Church, Paul now shows his preëminence in
view of his redeeming work. The nature of this work is
that of reconciliation; its means is the death of Christ;
its purpose is the holiness of believers; its human condi-

tion is faith. This paragraph (vs. 19–23) is bound to the preceding by the statement, "For it was the good pleasure of the Father that in him should all the fulness dwell." Only a divine Lord could be the Head of the Church. None but a divine Saviour could reconcile a world unto God.

Such seems to be the meaning and such the connection of these impressive words. "The fulness" denotes the sum total of the powers and attributes of God. All these are said to reside in Christ. The word "dwell" indicates not a temporary but a permanent residence. The indwelling of God in Christ is quite different from those shadowy and unreal and transient incarnations of which Oriental mystics dreamed and still dream. In Christ are embodied forever all the grace, the love, the wisdom, and the might of the eternal God.

This abiding "fulness" is due to "the good pleasure of the Father." It was the purpose of God and was well-pleasing to God that the divine nature in all its fullness should dwell in the Son. It made his saving work possible, and that work has its origin in the love and the grace of God.

The ultimate purpose of the Father was "to reconcile all things unto himself" through the work of his Son. This reconciliation meant the removal of all estrangements or barriers between God and men. The barriers included both the sinful impenitence of men and God's displeasure with sin. The difficulties on both sides were removed by the death of Christ, who "made peace through the blood of his cross." It is this cross which reveals the love of God, which touches the human heart and awakens a love for God and a desire to do his holy will. Man needed to be reconciled to God, but God took the initiative. In all the other religions of the world men are seeking God; in Christianity God is seeking men. He has undertaken the work of reconciliation. He has removed the obstacles. He has provided an atonement for sin. He has issued his appeal and he has sent forth the gospel messengers who beseech men, for Christ's sake, to be reconciled to God.

This reconciling work is intended for the whole universe.

It includes not only men and angels but "all things" as well, "whether things upon the earth, or things in the heavens." Just what is the scope of this universal reconciliation, or exactly what its details involve, it is impossible to affirm. The subject has been the occasion of endless discussion and conjecture. The main idea is clear and majestic. It is the purpose of God, in the gift of his Son, to abolish all the disorder of the universe and to bring into perfect and abiding harmony all powers and beings in heaven and on earth. Vs. 19, 20.

Paul now turns to a practical and personal application of the profound doctrines he is setting forth. He reminds the Colossians that they have a part in the divine reconciliation, and, further, that the aim of that reconciliation is moral perfection and its condition unwavering faith. It is of little value to the individual to read of a universal salvation unless he has a part personally in its blessed provision. Nor should one who regards himself as reconciled to God fail to strive to be well-pleasing to God or forget the necessity of unfaltering trust.

"And you, being in time past alienated and enemies in your mind in your evil works," writes the apostle as he describes the former condition of his Colossian readers. "In time past" they had been in a state of estrangement from God. They had been even hostile in their minds. Their hostility had resulted from their continual alienation and had been manifested in their "evil works." It was a hostility which was in the nature of willful opposition to a loving God, even of personal animosity to him. The seat of this antagonism was the mind; it was witnessed by wicked deeds. It had been so in the case of the Colossians; it is so with multitudes of men to-day.

It was not the mind of God that needed to be changed but the mind of man. God undertook the task and provided a means of reconciliation. This was in the death of Christ, or as Paul says, "In the body of his flesh through death." This same truth of reconciliation "through the blood of his cross" Paul had affirmed in the previous sentence. The unusual phrase, "Body of his flesh," has been supposed to be a reference to the Colossian heresy which taught the mediation of angels. It is probably better to see in it an emphasis upon the human nature of Christ as a necessary instrument in his reconciling work rather than an intentional allusion to any false doctrine. It was through the actual death of Christ upon the cross that God made his unique provision for bringing hostile souls into harmony and fellowship with himself. The ultimate purpose of God is the perfecting of human character. Thus Paul states, in the case of the Colossians, "You . . . hath he reconciled . . . to present you holy and without blemish and unreprovable before him." This moral and spiritual character, which it is the purpose of God to secure, is described first positively as "holy" and then negatively as "without blemish and unreprovable." Holiness denotes separation unto the service of God, definite consecration to him, and consequent moral purity. "Without blemish" indicates stainlessness of character and conduct. "Unreprovable" signifies "unblamable." Thus the character defined is absolutely pure and without blemish and without blame. It is so to appear when believers at last stand before the judgment seat of Christ, or when Christ finally shall have achieved his redeeming purpose to "present the church to himself a glorious church, not having spot or wrinkle or any such thing; but that it should be holy and without blemish."

Yet this future aspect of the divine purpose is not to be pressed too far. Paul has in mind both a prospect and a process. Perfection of character, as a result of the reconciliation effected by Christ, is being wrought out in this present life. It will be complete in the life to come. There is, however, one absolute condition. The believer must "continue in the faith, grounded and stedfast, and not moved away from the hope of the gospel."

Of this condition the Colossians sorely needed to be reminded. They were being beguiled by plausible heretics and threatened by undermining currents of false belief. Paul uses an expression which indicates his confidence in the Colossians yet at the same time emphasizes the fact that against every possible influence they must

adhere firmly to the gospel which they have "heard."
He employs the figure of a building. The foundation is
the gospel message which forms the substance of their
Christian faith. On that foundation the Colossians must
continue to be firmly "grounded," as a house which is
built upon a rock. They must be "stedfast," or built up
in such solid fashion as corresponds to a foundation so
secure. They must not be "moved away from the hope
of the gospel." Upon all the blessed assurances of holiness
and glory which the gospel contains they must stand
secure. "Stedfast" denotes strength of character. "Not
moved away" indicates stability of position, particularly
when withstanding influences which might dislodge. It is
even possible that Paul here changes the figure from that
of a building to that of a ship which might be "tossed to
and fro and carried about with every wind of doctrine."
If this sudden change is admitted, then the "hope of the
gospel" is the anchor which must not be allowed to drag.

To encourage this steadfast adherence to the true faith in
spite of opposing errors, Paul adds three phrases, all of
which refer to the gospel. He first tells his readers that
the faith which they must hold is the very gospel which
they have been taught, the very truth they "heard" first
from the lips of Epaphras. Of that gospel they know the
blessedness. The fruit of that faith has enriched their
lives. They need not concern themselves with new and
strange doctrines subversive of that faith.

If this interpretation lays too great stress upon the
words, "The gospel which ye heard," surely the next two
phrases are unquestionably arguments against surrender-
ing their faith because of the attacks of false teachers.
This gospel has been "preached in all creation under
heaven." This was not to be taken literally. In such a
context one need not demand "statistical exactness."
However, the gospel had been preached in every quarter
of the Roman Empire and its acceptance had been more
widespread than some readers may suppose. This universality of the gospel is presented by Paul as a guarantee
of its truth. The message which has been found to meet
the needs of all classes and races commends itself as being

a message from God.   Heresy is always local and provincial.   It usually appeals to one group of people or one
character of mind or one stage of culture.   What is believed by all Christians, in all places and at all times, one
need not hesitate to accept as true.

A third encouragement to adhere steadfastly to the
gospel is offered by the words, "Whereof I Paul was made
a minister."   The reference is obviously to the time of
Paul's conversion.   He had been a persecutor of Christians.   However, Christ, in his matchless grace, had
appeared to him and made him "a minister of the gospel."
This last phrase does not mean "the pastor of a church,"
or "a clergyman."   The word "minister" means "servant."   Paul had accepted Christ as his Lord, and had
been appointed by him to "serve" in the capacity of one
who proclaimed the gospel.   His marvelous conversion
should be to the Colossians a proof of the reality of the
faith they professed.   He reminds them that the gospel
they have heard, the gospel he himself preaches, is the very
gospel Christ commissioned him to proclaim.

This mention of his apostolic authority was designed to
emphasize his warning against the danger of apostasy;
however, it serves as a link between two portions of his
letter.   It introduces a fuller statement of the relation
his ministry sustains to the great truths of the Christian
faith and a more detailed reference to the speculative
errors which are imperiling the faith of his readers.

III. The Apostle of Christ.   Chs. 1:24 to 2:7

1. paul's service.   Ch. 1:24–29

24 Now I rejoice in my sufferings for your sake, and fill up on my part that which is lacking of the afflictions of Christ in my flesh for his body's sake, which is the church; 25 whereof I was made a minister, according to the dispensation of God which was given me to you-ward, to fulfil the word of God, 26 *even* the mystery which hath been hid for ages and generations: but now hath it been manifested to his saints, 27 to whom God was pleased to make known what is the riches of the glory of this mystery among the Gentiles, which is Christ in you, the hope of glory: 28 whom we proclaim, admonishing every man and teaching every man in all wisdom, that we may present every man perfect in Christ; 29 whereunto I labor also, striving according to his working, which worketh in me mightily.

Paul was always joyful. He had "learned, in whatsoever state . . . [he was], therein to be content." While a prisoner at Rome he wrote to the Philippians an epistle, the keynote of which is joy. During the same imprisonment he composed this letter to the Colossians. As he thinks of the glory of the gospel, and as he dwells upon his privilege of proclaiming the reconciling work of Christ, he can say, even while feeling the fetters upon his wrist, "Now I rejoice in my sufferings for your sake."

He has found, indeed, that the service in which he is engaged involves distress and pain. Yet he rejoices, not because of the sufferings but in spite of them; not on account of them but in the midst of them; for he realizes that they are endured for the benefit of the Church. They are "for your sake," he writes. In reality his sufferings were not directly connected with the Colossians. They had been incurred, however, in that wide ministry to the Gentile world as a result of which Epaphras had brought to Colossæ the "good news" of the gospel.

Ultimately, therefore, if not immediately, Paul suffered for the sake of these readers.

There is a further reason for his enduring these sufferings with joy. They supplement the sufferings of Christ. As Paul expresses it, they "fill up on my part that which is lacking of the afflictions of Christ in my flesh for his body's sake, which is the church." Unlike the actual sufferings of Christ, those of Paul were not atoning. They were on a different plane. They did not wash away sins. They did not expiate guilt. However, they were incurred in making known the redeeming work of Christ. They could add nothing to that finished work. Yet they were endured for the sake of Christ. They were like those of Christ, endured for the benefit of others. They thus united Paul with Christ. In this sense they were supplementary to "the afflictions of Christ." In this sense they were part of "the afflictions of Christ."

More specifically still, they are endured for the sake of the Church and in the service of the Church. As Christ endured bodily sufferings, so has Paul endured, and the physical sufferings of Paul are for the benefit of the spiritual body of Christ, which is the Church. It is with this fact in mind that Paul can rejoice in his sufferings, in behalf of the Church whereof, writes the apostle, he "was made a minister."

The ministry does not refer to the duties of a local church officer. It describes the wide service which Paul was rendering in making known the gospel of Christ. This was in the nature of a "stewardship"—for thus many prefer to render the word "dispensation." Paul was a servant in the household of God, and to him had been intrusted the sacred treasure of the gospel. It was not to be enjoyed by himself alone, nor to be shared only with his people, the Jews. It was for the Gentile world as well, and thus for the Colossians, or, as Paul says, "Which was given me to you-ward."

If the word "dispensation," or "divine ordering," is preferred, the meaning is much the same. The conversion and mission of Paul were in accordance with the gracious purpose of God which had in view the preaching of the gospel in all the world. Only by thus including the Gentiles could this purpose be achieved. Only thus would it be possible "to fulfil the word of God," that is, to give full effect to the message which God had sent to men.

This "word of God" Paul proceeds to describe as "the mystery which hath been hid for ages and generations." The word "mystery" is not to be connected with the beliefs or practices of the ancient mystery religions. It had been a common word for "secret." In the New Testament it is used to describe something once concealed but now revealed. It denotes, not something which men are hiding from their fellow men, but something which could never have been known by men had it not been for a divine revelation or disclosure. It is not something which is hard to be understood, or which must be kept secret, but a reality which God has revealed so that it may be proclaimed to all the world.

Thus Paul declares the gospel to be a "mystery" which was unknown in time past, or which God only imperfectly or partially had revealed, "but now hath it been manifested to his saints." The word "saints" is used to describe Christians in general, who are regarded as "the people of God," persons separated unto the service of God.

To these "saints," through no merit of their own, but by the grace and will of God, this mystery has been made known in all its glory. Paul states it thus: "To whom God was pleased to make known what is the riches of the glory of this mystery among the Gentiles." The full wealth of the divine mercy and goodness has been revealed in the inclusion of the Gentile peoples of all the world in the saving purpose of God. It was in the mission to the Gentile world, intrusted first to Paul, that the universality and full glory of the gospel was made known.

The essence of this "mystery," the center of the gospel, is Christ—"Which is Christ in you," writes the apostle, "the hope of glory." The words may be translated, "Christ in you," or, "Christ among you." The Christ who was preached as Saviour "among the Gentiles," the Christ who was working in the Gentile as well as in the Jewish world, or the Christ who, as a living presence, was

dwelling in the Colossian believers—this Christ is himself
the Pledge and Assurance, the living Hope, of the glorious
immortality awaiting those who put their trust in him.

It is such a Christ that Paul has been sent to proclaim,
and his aim he declares to be the moral perfection of
believers—"Whom we proclaim," he writes, "admonishing every man and teaching every man in all wisdom."
He indicates that the two chief functions of the preacher
are, "warning," or reproving or convincing of error, and
"teaching," or instructing in the faith. This preaching,
therefore, is summarized in the words "repent" and
"believe," but must also include due instruction in moral
principles and practice. The manner and method of this
admonishing and teaching is to be "in all wisdom." The
gospel may appear simple in its essence, but it contains
depths which no mind can fathom. It is really more
profound than all the boasted philosophies of false teachers. Its rightful presentation requires a wisdom which
the Spirit alone can give.

The aim in preaching, however, is intensely practical.
It is, as Paul states, to "present every man perfect in
Christ." Three times Paul repeats the words, "Every
man." To him the gospel was universal, but he saw the
need of personal dealing with individuals. His hope and
goal is to present finally, at the judgment seat of Christ, in
complete perfection of nature, everyone who has been
within the sphere of his influence. This can be attained
not merely through the power of the preacher but by
divine strength, and only as the believer is in vital union
with Christ.

Effort is needed, however, on the part of the preacher.
"Whereunto I labor also," writes the apostle, employing
an expression which denotes toil carried to the point of
weariness or exhaustion, "striving according to his working, which worketh in me mightily." This "striving," or
"agonizing," indicates the most strenuous and self-denying
effort. Such toil and strain are made possible, however,
and are accomplished by the power of Christ. It is really
a divine energy which is working in and through the apostle.

Such, then, is the part Paul has in the proclamation of

the gospel. His sufferings are for the Church. V. 24.
His message is the "mystery" of Christ. Vs. 25–27. His
aim is the perfection of everyone who accepts the gospel.
V. 28. His strength is imparted by the Lord whom he
trusts and serves. V. 29.

2. PAUL'S SOLICITUDE.   Ch. 2:1–7

1 For I would have you know how greatly I strive for you,
and for them at Laodicea, and for as many as have not seen
my face in the flesh; 2 that their hearts may be comforted,
they being knit together in love, and unto all riches of the full
assurance of understanding, that they may know the mystery
of God, *even* Christ, 3 in whom are all the treasures of wisdom
and knowledge hidden.   4 This I say, that no one may delude
you with persuasiveness of speech. 5 For though I am absent
in the flesh, yet am I with you in the spirit, joying and beholding your order, and the stedfastness of your faith in Christ.

6 As therefore ye received Christ Jesus the Lord, *so* walk
in him, 7 rooted and builded up in him, and established in
your faith, even as ye were taught, abounding in thanksgiving.

Among the many burdens which daily pressed upon the
heart of Paul was one which he described as "anxiety
for all the churches," II Cor. 11:28. This care extended
not only to the churches he had founded but also to those
established by the effort and influence of his messengers
and friends. Such was the case with those of the Lycos
Valley, in the cities of Laodicea and Hierapolis and
Colossæ.

"For I would have you know," writes the apostle,
"how greatly I strive for you, and for them at Laodicea,
and for as many as have not seen my face in the flesh."
In the previous paragraph he has stated the strenuous
character of his ministry; here he gives a specific instance.
There he referred to his outward activities; here he reveals
the anxieties and struggles of his soul.

These latter he would not conceal. He wishes his
readers to "know" and appreciate them. It may lead
them to realize the seriousness of their situation and the
peril in which they stand. His desire, as he expresses it, is
to "have you know how greatly I strive for you," or as

his words may be rendered, "What a strain I have to carry in my care for you." The reference is to the inner strain of anxiety, or prayer, or yearning desire.

This was felt for the Colossian Christians, but also for those in the neighboring church of Laodicea, and indeed for all who had not seen his face in the flesh. That the last phrase includes the former, and that Paul had never visited these cities of the Lycos Valley, seems clear from a study of his life as contained in The Acts and in his own Epistles.

That for which the apostle so anxiously yearned is expressed in the phrases which follow. "That their hearts may be comforted" means not consoled merely, but strengthened. The word here denotes "not relief but reënforcement." Their minds and wills as well as their emotions were included in the term "hearts."

The Colossians did not need comfort in sorrow but rather confirmation in faith. This confirmation is defined as a closer unity in love, a deepening of conviction, and a fuller knowledge of Christ.

Thus it is the deep concern of Paul that the Colossian believers may be strengthened in faith, "being knit together in love." In the next chapter of the epistle love is called "the bond of perfectness." It is the ideal link by which men are united. Such a union will result in attaining the spiritual wealth which consists in an unwavering certitude taking complete possession of the understanding or judgment. This insight into spiritual truth, this deep conviction and confidence, is described by Paul as the "riches of the full assurance of understanding." It is further specified as consisting in a full knowledge of Christ: "That they may know the mystery of God, even Christ."

The word "mystery" has its usual New Testament meaning. It describes something once hidden but now disclosed—something, too, which is not to be kept secret but which is to be made known. Christ, in his person and work, in his coming and his character, is such a "mystery." He is the supreme and essential revelation. He is the Son of God, the eternal Word, "the light of the world."

Paul adds, "In whom are all the treasures of wisdom

and knowledge hidden." The distinction between "wisdom" and "knowledge" is not quite certain. Probably "wisdom" is to be regarded as the larger and higher term. "Knowledge" refers to the apprehending of truths; "wisdom" to the power of reasoning about them and applying them to life. Knowledge is "information"; wisdom is also "inspiration." Paul is insisting that the whole wealth of spiritual insight which men need, the beliefs concerning God which they should hold, and the laws of conduct by which they are to be guided are all stored up for them in Christ.

They are "hidden" in Christ as in a treasure house—but in the sense that they are so concealed that they can be shared by those who are willing to make an effort to secure them. Those who seek will find. Nor should one seek for these "treasures of wisdom and knowledge" in any other place than in Christ. "All" are in him. Yet one who would possess these treasures must be earnest in his endeavor to know Christ and serious in his thought and meditation upon the truths revealed in him. More and more fully can Christ be known. Larger and larger are those priceless stores which must be sought and can be found in him. No other revelation of God is needed, but in Christ are boundless riches yet undiscovered by his Church.

Paul lays this stress upon his solicitude for the Colossian Christians and upon his desire that they may attain a complete knowledge of Christ, because he is about to warn them against the false teachers who were attempting to beguile them by their proud boasts of superior wisdom: "This I say, that no one may delude you with persuasiveness of speech." Their danger, then, was that of being deceived both by the plausible arguments of the heretics who were threatening the Church and also by their suave language. They were in peril of accepting doctrines as true without understanding their real nature and consequences.

As yet they had not been deluded. Paul implies no censure. He is about to expose the specious errors which threatened them. Thus with extreme delicacy and wisdom he prepares the way for his warning by a warm expression of confidence and an encouraging admonition.

"For though I am absent in the flesh, yet am I with you in the spirit," writes Paul, vividly imagining himself present with these friends whom he has never seen, but for whom he feels a loving sympathy, "joying and beholding your order, and the stedfastness of your faith in Christ." The "order" of the Colossian church, which gave Paul such joy, refers to the unity of faith which bound the members together like an army in an "orderly array." Their "stedfastness" indicated the "firmness" of their faith, or, the "solid front" which they presented in the face of the opposing errors. Thus it is evident that the church as a whole stood true to the gospel it had received.

That it may remain true to this gospel is the sum of the exhortation which follows: "As therefore ye received Christ Jesus the Lord, so walk in him, rooted and builded up in him, and established in your faith, even as ye were taught, abounding in thanksgiving."

The first general command, then, is to conform their lives to their early Christian instruction. The word "as" is important, and implies the "so" which the translators supply. The Colossians were to maintain the form of doctrine that they had been taught by Epaphras. From him they had learned to regard Jesus as the true Messiah, the Saviour, their Lord, the complete revelation of God, "the mystery . . . in whom are all the treasures of wisdom and knowledge hidden." They not only had accepted these truths about Christ; they had "received Christ Jesus the Lord" into their hearts and lives. They now must not think of abandoning him, but must remain constant in their devotion. They had "received" him as "the Christ of prophecy, the Jesus of history, the Lord of life."

To this gospel message, to this divine Christ, their course or manner of life must conform. They must "walk in him." Step by step they must move forward in vital union with him. The mode of this life Paul proceeds to define further in swiftly changing metaphors. They are to "walk" as men, but also to be "rooted" like trees, and to be "builded up" like a house. The tenses of the Greek participles are of interest. They have been "rooted" once for all; they are being "builded up" continuously.

When they received Christ the roots of life were planted deep in him; they should remain there undisturbed. Their lives rested upon Christ as on a sure foundation; upon that foundation they must let them be built up stage by stage.

Furthermore, they were to be continually "established" in the faith which they, at the outset, had been taught, or strengthened in the belief which had been theirs since first they learned of Christ. Faith should be developed. Its scope should be enlarged. Its sight should become more clear. Yet progress does not consist in abandoning established truths and accepting speculative vagaries.

Last of all, Paul urges upon his readers the duty of "abounding in thanksgiving" as the natural expression of a vital faith. Such constant gratitude will be called forth by keeping in mind the boundless benefits received through Christ, and will result in lives yielded to him in joyful service and strong to resist all influences which might incline them to disloyalty or doubt.

IV. THE FALSE PHILOSOPHY AND THE TRUE FAITH.
Chs. 2:8 to 3:4

1. THE SUFFICIENCY OF CHRIST.   Ch. 2:8–15

8 Take heed lest there shall be any one that maketh spoil of you through his philosophy and vain deceit, after the tradition of men, after the rudiments of the world, and not after Christ: 9 for in him dwelleth all the fulness of the Godhead bodily, 10 and in him ye are made full, who is the head of all principality and power: 11 in whom ye were also circumcised with a circumcision not made with hands, in the putting off of the body of the flesh, in the circumcision of Christ; 12 having been buried with him in baptism, wherein ye were also raised with him through faith in the working of God, who raised him from the dead.   13 And you, being dead through your trespasses and the uncircumcision of your flesh, you, *I say*, did he make alive together with him, having forgiven us all our trespasses; 14 having blotted out the bond written in ordinances that was against us, which was contrary to us: and he hath taken it out of the way, nailing it to the cross; 15 having despoiled the principalities and the powers, he made a show of them openly, triumphing over them in it.

This section of the epistle, chs. 2:8 to 3:4, is properly designated as "polemical," in contrast with the preceding paragraphs which are "doctrinal," chs. 1:15 to 2:7, and the following section, chs. 3:5 to 4:6, which is described as "practical." The term "polemical," however, is not wholly felicitous. It often implies severity or unfairness in controversy. Then, too, this "polemical" section contains much that is doctrinal and also much that is practical. However, it is here that Paul does attack the false teachers that were troubling the Colossian church. At least this section embodies the warning against error which constitutes the essential message of the epistle.

A warning, however kindly intended, may be so worded as to cause offense. Paul was not guilty of this fault.

He introduced his warning by a generous expression of confidence, v. 5, and a message of kindly encouragement, vs. 6, 7.

Furthermore, in his solemn caution to the Colossians, Paul shows how heresy best may be met. It is not by bitter denunciation, nor yet by detailed discussion of the false doctrines, but by positive affirmation of the truth. Thus in this letter, written specifically to correct erroneous teaching, nothing has been said, so far, as to the heresy at Colossæ, but a notable statement has been made as to the unique preëminence of Christ. Thus, too, when he now reaches the very heart of his letter the apostle dwells so eloquently upon the deity of Christ and the dignity and completeness of believers that the reader is left in some uncertainty as to the exact system of error against which the Colossians were to be upon their guard.

This much is beyond question: The heresy which threatened the Colossians was Jewish. Its advocates sought to bind upon Christian believers the Hebrew ceremonial, with its rites and feasts and fasts. It was also ascetic and taught the neglect or the abuse of the body. Furthermore, it was mystical. It included the worship of imaginary angelic beings and embodied elements of Oriental mysticism, while exhibiting the proud pretensions which characterize systems of occult science.

"Take heed," writes the apostle, "lest there shall be any one that maketh spoil of you through his philosophy and vain deceit." To "make spoil" means to "carry away captive." It presents the picture of those long lines of wretched prisoners of war who were led away into slavery by Oriental conquerors. The Colossians had been delivered "out of the power of darkness, and translated . . . into the kingdom" of Christ. They were now in danger of losing their liberty and of being again enslaved.

The instrument used by the enemy is described as "philosophy and vain deceit," or as the phrase probably means, "A so-called 'philosophy' which is a vain deceit." This is the only place in the Bible where the word "philosophy" occurs. It originally was a modest expression denoting "love of wisdom." Those sages who first used it hesitated to call themselves "wise men"; they were merely "lovers of wisdom" or "philosophers." Later the word acquired real dignity and implied a reasoned view of life or of the universe. However, as used by the Colossian heretics to describe their system, it implied that they possessed vast stores of truth which Christian believers did not share. Paul declares that this boasted wisdom is merely a "vain deceit," an empty delusion.

True philosophy Paul could not fail to respect. This false philosophy he continues to expose. He declares that it is "after the tradition of men." A tradition may be valuable. It means something "handed down" from generation to generation. If, however, it has no basis in reality; if its source is mere human speculation; most of all, if it displaces divine revelation, then it is worthless and dangerous and harmful. So Christ rebuked the Pharisees by saying, "Ye leave the commandment of God, and hold fast the tradition of men," Mark 7:8. This was the exact fault of the heretical leaders. This temptation is common in every age, namely, to substitute human theories for divine realities.

The Colossian heresy is further described as being "after the rudiments of the world." This phrase probably applies to the Jewish ceremonials which the false teachers were attempting to bind upon the consciences of the Colossians. Many modern scholars, who find in the Colossian heresy rather elaborate elements of Gnosticism and angelolatry, are inclined to identify these "rudiments of the world" with the "elemental spirits" which in pagan and later Jewish belief were associated with wind, cold, heat, and all natural phenomena. "The rudiments of the world," therefore, would mean "the angelic beings supposed to be in control of the universe."

However, the use of the phrase in Gal. 4:3, and the fact that here it is followed by the references to "circumcision," Col. 2:11, 13, and to feast days and Sabbath Days, v. 16, and also the connection with Jewish "ordinances" in which the phrase is repeated, v. 20, indicate that it may be sufficient to find in the words a designation of the ritual observances of the Jews. They are here called "rudiments," because they belonged to an elementary and preparatory system of religious teaching. They are "of the world," belonging to the sphere of the outward and material as opposed to the realm of the spiritual. Such ceremonies and rites were adapted to an age of religious immaturity. To return to these would be distinct retrogression.

Whatever the exact meaning of the "tradition" or the "rudiments" embodied in the false philosophy of the heretical leaders, the serious indictment against them both was this: namely, they were "not after Christ." They took men away from Christ. They weakened faith in Christ. They stood in the way of Christ. This is condemnation enough for any system of teaching or for any proud philosophy.

We may not be able to discover the exact form of the Colossian heresy. This is not important. What is really important is the warning that any human theories or any views of life and the world which deny the claims of Christ, or take men away from Christ, or deny to Christ his place of supreme, unique, divine supremacy, can be accepted only at the price of spiritual peril and immeasurable loss.

"For in him dwelleth all the fulness of the Godhead bodily." This is the reason why the Colossians were to be on their guard against any vain philosophy that might turn them away from Christ by its human tradition, by its attractive ritual, or by its reverence for any imagined angelic beings.

"In him" is emphatic. It is in Christ, and nowhere else, that one is to find "the fulness of the Godhead." In him the fullness "dwelleth," that is, has its permanent abode. This "fulness" means the unbounded powers and attributes of God. The word "Godhead" denotes the essence or content of divine being, that indeed which constitutes God. Here in most absolute terms Paul states not merely the divinity but the deity of Christ. The word deity, and its corresponding word in the Greek, denotes the "being God." Christ is not only Godlike; he is God. It is the distinction which finally was made between "ὁμοιούσιος," meaning a nature like the Father's, and "ὁμοούσιος," meaning the same nature as the Father's, or "Being of one substance with the Father," as The Nicene Creed declared. The Nicene controversy was more than a quarrel over a letter. It was a choice between a Saviour who was a man and a Saviour who is God.

This fullness of the divine nature dwells in Christ "bodily," that is, "in bodily form." This is a clear statement of incarnation. In the glorified bodily form of Christ all the plenitude of deity permanently dwells. Nor is this statement a speculative dogma. It is a practical truth, for Paul adds, "And in him ye are made full." Just because the fullness of deity dwells in Christ, therefore believers, by abiding in him, receive the fullness of their spiritual life. In him every want is supplied. This surely does not mean that Christians become partakers of deity. They do not share the essence or the attributes of God. Omniscience and omnipotence and omnipresence are not theirs. It does not even intimate that Christians are morally perfect. It does denote that in Christ they have a source from which flows all needed grace and courage and wisdom and strength. The process is gradual. By abiding in Christ it may be continuous. Up to the measure of human capacity, up to the limit of ideal human destiny, Christians are made partakers of that divine life of beauty and holiness and love which in its fullness dwells in Christ.

They need to seek no other source of grace. They can show allegiance and submission to no other spiritual beings, for Christ "is the head of all principality and power." Least of all need they place reliance upon the Jewish ordinances and ceremonies advocated by the false teachers. The typical rite was that of circumcision. The reality corresponding to that symbol had already been experienced. By accepting Christ, by abandoning their sins, by their spiritual renewal, they had received the true circumcision. They had been, as Paul declares, "circumcised with a circumcision not made with hands, in the putting off of the body of the flesh, in the circumcision of Christ."

Instead of the old, Christians had adopted a new rite, namely, baptism. It symbolized not only the putting off of sinful habits and passions, but actual death to a former life of evil, and also resurrection to a new life of purity and holiness. This death and this resurrection were made possible by Christ. Faith in him was expressed in baptism, and by faith believers experienced a spiritual change as real and as marvelous as that which God wrought in raising Christ from the dead. This spiritual resurrection Paul thus describes: "Having been buried with him in baptism, wherein ye were also raised with him through faith in the working of God, who raised him from the dead," v. 12.

This moral renewal not only Jews but also Gentiles had experienced. The Colossians, who once had been spiritually dead in sins, and whose uncircumcision was a symbol of their enmity against God, had likewise experienced a spiritual resurrection by faith in Christ: "And you, being dead through your trespasses and the uncircumcision of your flesh, you, I say, did he make alive together with him."

This gift of a new life is associated by Paul with another act on the part of God, a gracious bestowal accepted by faith, namely, forgiveness of sins: "Having forgiven us all our trespasses." The pronoun is here changed from "you" to "us." Paul thus gracefully associates himself with his readers; he gratefully acknowledges his part in the pardoning grace of God.

Such pardon was necessary. All had been under condemnation. Against Jew and Gentile alike there was a bond, a note unpaid, an obligation unfulfilled. This bond was the law of God, chiefly the law embodied in the Ten Commandments, but also, for the Gentiles, the law of conscience "written in their hearts." This bond Christ canceled by his atoning death, "having blotted out the bond written in ordinances that was against us, which was contrary to us: and he hath taken it out of the way, nailing it to the cross," v. 14.

This death of Christ was not only a pardon; it also manifested might. It not only canceled a debt; it was a glorious triumph. By his cross the mighty Victor defeated

Satan and all his hosts; he despoiled them of their armor; he put them to open shame; he led them captive in triumph: "Having despoiled the principalities and the powers, he made a show of them openly, triumphing over them in it." Why, then, fear the spiritual powers or the angelic beings before whom the false teachers bowed in worship? Why submit to Jewish rites and ceremonies? Christ alone is the Saviour. He is supreme. In him is life. He meets our every need.

2. A TWOFOLD WARNING. Ch. 2:16–19

16 Let no man therefore judge you in meat, or in drink, or in respect of a feast day or a new moon or a sabbath day: 17 which are a shadow of the things to come; but the body is Christ's. 18 Let no man rob you of your prize by a voluntary humility and worshipping of the angels, dwelling in the things which he hath seen, vainly puffed up by his fleshly mind, 19 and not holding fast the Head, from whom all the body, being supplied and knit together through the joints and bands, increaseth with the increase of God.

In view of the believers' sufficiency in Christ, vs. 8–15, Paul proceeds to warn the Colossians against an enslaving ritualism, vs. 16, 17, and also against a false mysticism, vs. 18, 19. It is not wrong to use a ritual. Symbols and ceremonies may awake emotion, may stimulate thought, may strengthen faith. They may be precious vehicles for conveying divine truth. However, when they have served their specific purpose they may become meaningless, and if they are put in the place of the living Christ they may be dangerous or injurious.

The latter was the peril at Colossæ. The false teachers were attempting to bind upon the consciences of Christian believers the rites of Judaism. Against this Paul protests: "Let no man therefore judge you in meat, or in drink, or in respect of a feast day or a new moon or a sabbath day." The "therefore" refers the reader back to the preceding paragraph. There it had been asserted that the believer finds in Christ the divine supply of all his spiritual needs. He has been given a new life. He has received all that the Jewish law symbolized; he has been set free from all its demands. "Therefore," writes the apostle, "let no man . . . judge you"—let no man take you to task—"in meat, or in drink," that is, in the matter of eating or drinking. The reference is to Jewish regulations as to clean and unclean food and other restrictions of diet, which were being made even more stringent by the Colossian heretics. "Or in respect of a feast day or a new moon or a sabbath day," continues the apostle as he insists further upon Christian liberty from Mosaic institutions. A follower of Christ is not bound by the necessity of observing the sacred seasons of the Jews, whether annual festivals, such as passover and pentecost and tabernacles, or monthly holy days, or the narrowly restricted weekly "sabbath."

The ground of such Christian liberty is found in the fact that these regulations and observances were prophetic and preparatory and therefore no longer to be required of the people of God. "Which are a shadow of the things to come," writes Paul; "but the body is Christ's."

The Mosaic institutions were of great value. They set forth the need of holiness, of pardon, of purity. They pointed to a great High Priest and to a perfect atonement. They contained a promise of fellowship with God. They symbolized the rest and peace of a true spiritual experience. Yet they constituted only a "shadow"; the real substance is in Christ and within the gift of Christ: "The body is Christ's." In him can be found, and from him can be received, all the blessings typified by the ceremonials of the Jews.

Since these ceremonials were mere shadows and have been superseded, it may be concluded that they must be abandoned. Paul does not so argue. He is much more tolerant. He leaves the decision to each Christian. It was a time of transition. Christians were allowed to choose. What Paul does insist, however, is that no one shall be compelled to observe a form or a ceremony. "Let no man therefore judge you" in these matters, Paul insists. Tastes and temperaments differ. Observances which help some persons may not be of service to

others. However, when some one insists that certain
ceremonials must be observed, when he declares that his
forms of worship are necessary to salvation, then he must
be resisted, in the interests of Christian liberty and of truth.
Christ alone is the Author of salvation. Faith in him is
the sole essential. To insist upon the necessity of a rite
or ceremony is to displace Christ and to deny his claims.
Let no one substitute a "shadow," forgetting that "the
body is Christ's."   Vs. 16, 17.

The Colossian heresy was essentially Jewish. However, there is no question that it had elements of an Oriental
mysticism which centered in the worship of angels. In the
highest sense of the words there is a true "Christian
mysticism." In all reality Paul was a mystic. He believed that in Christ he had found a complete revelation
and real vision of God such as human reason could not
attain, and that through Christ he had immediate and
direct intercourse with God.

There have always been mystics of a very different
character. They make claims to supernatural visions and
revelations. They profess to communicate with unseen
spirits. They glory in systems of occult science. They
claim a direct knowledge of the divine which only the
initiated can attain.

Such were the false mystics against whom Paul warns
the Colossians. He describes them in four graphic
phrases. "Let no man rob you of your prize," he writes,
referring to the Christian's immortal crown, "by a voluntary humility and worshipping of the angels." These
mystics were characterized then, first of all, by a species of
mock "humility." It was "voluntary" and self-conscious,
and thus unreal. It was expressed in "worshipping . . .
angels" as the representatives of God, and was thus alleged
to be less presumptuous than the direct worship of God,
as though he were too high to be worshiped by men. Yet
to refuse God's appointed way of approach through Christ
was really presumptuous pride.

In the second phrase one of these mystics is described
as "dwelling in the things which he hath seen."   This ref-

erence to alleged visions contains probably a touch of
irony. Paul indicates that the pretended revelations on
which this false teacher laid much store were unreal;
he was living in a world of hallucinations and self-
deceptions. This fairly describes most leaders of occult
science, of theosophy, and esoteric systems of belief.

The next phrase pictures the unwarranted conceit of
the proud mystic. Claiming a superior spiritual and intellectual insight, he is declared to be "vainly puffed up by
his fleshly mind." By "vainly" Paul means "without
reason" or "without ground." He is "puffed up" or in-
flated by his senseless pride. His boasted insight is
"fleshly" and carnal. Therefore, instead of having attained a higher level, his intelligence is dominated by that
which is material and secular and unspiritual.

The last fault of the heretic teacher is the worst. It
may have been the cause or possibly the result of the
other three. He is described as "not holding fast the
Head." His dependence upon ceremonies or his mystical
speculation as to superhuman spirits had resulted in his
losing his grasp upon Christ. This is inevitable. It is
far too common. Such a loss is fatal. Only by "holding
fast the Head" can one attain a deeper spiritual insight,
or more vigorous spiritual life; for it is Christ "from whom
all the body, being supplied and knit together through the
joints and bands, increaseth with the increase of God."
Thus two results of holding fast to Christ are noted: first,
unity and, second, sustenance. Both these were being
sacrificed by the trusting in a ritual and by the "worshipping of the angels." The Colossian heretic was claiming a great spiritual advance; but in reality he was growing
spiritually weak. He was proud of his little coterie of
intellectual aristocrats; he actually was severing himself
from the Body of Christ.

This familiar figure of the Body emphasizes here both
the unity and the diversity in the life of the Church. All
who trust Christ belong to the one Body of which he is
the Head. Yet in this Body there are many different
members, many "joints and bands" through which the
divine life flows. When every member holds fast to Christ,

and is thus supplied with strength and is united with
the other members, then "all the body . . . increaseth
with the increase of God." It is an increase which comes
from God and is of the nature of God. The life of the
true Church, both its source and its character, is divine.
It is therefore evident why Paul so earnestly warns the
Colossians against any ritual observance or mystic speculation which might lessen their allegiance to Christ. Vs.
18, 19.

3. A TWOFOLD EXHORTATION.   Chs. 2:20 to 3:4

20 If ye died with Christ from the rudiments of the world,
why, as though living in the world, do ye subject yourselves
to ordinances, 21 Handle not, nor taste, nor touch 22 (all
which things are to perish with the using), after the precepts
and doctrines of men? 23 Which things have indeed a show
of wisdom in will-worship, and humility, and severity to the
body; *but are* not of any value against the indulgence of the
flesh.
Ch. 3:1 If then ye were raised together with Christ, seek
the things that are above, where Christ is, seated on the right
hand of God. 2 Set your mind on the things that are above,
not on the things that are upon the earth. 3 For ye died,
and your life is hid with Christ in God. 4 When Christ, *who
is* our life, shall be manifested, then shall ye also with him
be manifested in glory.

Paul is arguing against the false teaching at Colossæ.
In contrast with their insistence upon Jewish rites and
mystic doctrines he has insisted upon the sufficiency and
supremacy of Christ. With this in view he gave a twofold warning. Upon this he now bases a twofold exhortation. The death of Christ annulled all the law's demands;
the resurrection of Christ assures new life for the believer.
Faith unites the Christian with Christ both in his death
and in his life. Thus these exhortations are based upon
the two facts of the believer's fellowship, first in the cross
and second in the resurrection of his Lord. "If ye died
with Christ" is the assumption of the first, vs. 20–23.
"If then ye were raised together with Christ" is the foundation of the second, ch. 3:1–4.

It is hardly necessary to note that Paul is dealing here with the Colossian heresy, the essence of which was an endeavor to compel Christians to practice the ceremonies of the Jewish law. The restrictions of the law seem to have been made more stringent by the false teachers and to have become decidedly ascetic in character. Paul here insists that in the light of the cross such restrictions and practices are faithless and futile.

They are faithless because in accepting Christ as a Saviour the believer professed to have died to the old system of shadows and symbols and to have found in Christ the fulfillment of all that the Mosaic Law had been designed to typify and to predict. "If ye died with Christ from the rudiments of the world," writes the apostle. The "if" does not imply uncertainty. The phrase is intended to state unquestioned fact. "Since ye died with Christ," or, "Inasmuch as ye died with Christ," is what is meant. The time of this death was in the past. It was when, at baptism, faith in Christ had been confessed and when Christ had been accepted as Master and Lord. "At that time," Paul indicates, "ye died . . . from the rudiments of the world." These believers had then been separated from those elementary forms of religious instruction, those Jewish rites and ceremonies, which had been fulfilled in Christ and thus been superseded by Christ. "Why," asks the apostle, "[with what reason, with what excuse] as though living in the world, do ye subject yourselves to ordinances?" They professed to have left that old world of rules and regulations; why now should they voluntarily submit themselves to the tyranny of these outworn and abandoned systems of outward forms? These ordinances are defined by terms quoted from the lips of the false teachers: "Handle not, nor taste, nor touch." These prohibitions applied to the eating of certain kinds of food and also to contact with things regarded as ceremonially unclean.

For several reasons, Paul shows, these outworn prohibitions are futile for a Christian. They attach eternal significance to things which "are to perish with the using."

They are concerned with what is material and transient and can have no bearing on the destiny of immortal souls.

Then again these prohibitions are "after the precepts and doctrines of men." They are mere human ordinances and are not to be accepted by those who have professed Christ to be their only Master and Lord.

The chief objection of the apostle, however, is that these ordinances fail in their alleged purpose. They do not result in restraining one from evil. They "have . . . a show of wisdom," or "an apparent justification," on the ground of "will-worship," or the proud observance of a self-imposed ritual. Their advocates thus make an officious parade of their devotion. They manifest an assumed "humility" which is not real but is a mere affectation. They also practice severe bodily austerity. Yet both legalism and asceticism fail at the same point. In spite of all their "show of wisdom," these ordinances and severities "are not of any value against the indulgence of the flesh." That is the test and the condemnation of every false system. It fails to make men better. It is powerless to withstand evil desires and appetites. It gives no victory over the lower nature. If religion is a matter of mere ceremonial or self-denials and restrictions, it is morally impotent. All manner of vices may flourish under its shadow. The spirit can overcome the flesh only by the power of the living Christ. Ch. 2:20–23.

Resurrection quite as truly as crucifixion is used by Paul as a symbol of spiritual experience. One who is united with Christ by a living faith is pictured as having both "died with Christ" and having been "raised together with Christ." The death is negative; the resurrection is positive. One looks to the past; the other to the present and future. The former points to the end of a previous manner of life; the latter indicates what the life has begun to be.

Thus when Paul has reminded the Colossians that by faith they have "died with Christ" to ceremonies and ascetic rites as means of moral attainment, he exhorts them, on the ground that they "were raised together with

Christ," to seek for spiritual progress by fixing their minds upon the risen and ascended Lord.

This exhortation to "seek the things that are above," considered quite apart from its connection, is easily understood and forms a paragraph of extraordinary beauty. However, when taken in its context, its meaning is made more clear and its significance greatly enhanced. It is seen to be the climax and conclusion of that whole section of the epistle in which Paul has been dealing with the false teaching at Colossæ. Ch. 2:8–13. It is likewise the source and summary of those practical precepts which constitute the following portion of the letter. Chs. 3:5 to 4:6. These precepts merely enjoin, in the various spheres of duty, the manifestation of the life which issues from death and resurrection with Christ.

"If then ye were raised together with Christ," writes the apostle. The word "if" implies no uncertainty and no question. It is rather intended to state a great truth, namely, "Ye were raised together with Christ." This is indeed a supreme reality. By faith in Christ believers have died to an old world of sin and of self, of ceremonies and of rites, and they have risen to a new life of holiness and service, of purity and beauty and love.

If this is true, and it is, why then think of turning to that low plane of Jewish ceremonial and ascetic practices on which the false teachers are standing? Rather, "seek the things that are above," the things which belong to that higher sphere, "where Christ is," the risen and ascended Christ, who occupies the place of supreme power, "seated on the right hand of God." These things are to be the objects for which the believer is striving, the goal he is seeking to attain. As realized in actual life, these things are not vague and shadowy and mystical. They consist of those virtues which Paul proceeds to describe. Vs. 12–17. They are manifested in sympathy and meekness and love, in the "peace of Christ," in the "word of Christ," in all that is done in the "name of the Lord Jesus." They are to be experienced, not merely in some distant heaven, but here on earth, in the Christian household, in the relations of wives and husbands, of children and parents, of servants and masters. Ch. 3:18 to 4:1.

On these things as related to Christ, on these things as regulated by Christ, on these things "set your mind," fix your thoughts. Let these be the objects of your longing. "Not on the things that are upon the earth," does not imply a life of dreamy and sentimental inactivity. The attitude of heart and mind which is centered upon the risen, omnipotent Christ results in the most strenuous endeavor and active service in every sphere of human relationship. It brings to bear the most heavenly motives upon the most humble duties. None of "the things that are upon the earth" are to be neglected or despised, except in so far as they stand between the soul and Christ, or make one unmindful of Christ. If they do, then they are to be dismissed from the thought; they are not then to be the object of the Christian's desire—"for ye died." When you accepted Christ as a Saviour you turned not only from sins, but from ceremonies as a means of pleasing God and from "things that are upon the earth" as the means of satisfying the immortal soul.

"Your death to all those things of earth has resulted in a higher life," Paul is indicating. It is a life linked with Christ in all its aims and purposes and hopes. It is a mysterious life. Men whose motives and goals and principles are of the "earth" cannot understand it or appreciate it. "Your life is hid with Christ in God." Just as the risen Christ is hidden now in the life of God, so those who belong to Christ are hidden from the comprehension of the world. They are misinterpreted, misrepresented. The source of their strength, the nature of their joys, the cause of their peace, are all a mystery.

The explanation of the mystery is given by Paul for himself and for all his fellow believers when he refers to "Christ, who is our life." The life of one who lives with Christ, who lives for Christ, who lives in Christ must be a hidden life. However, as Christ some day is to reappear, so these hidden lives are some day to be revealed in their real nature, are to be manifested, are to be understood.

"When Christ, who is our life, shall be manifested, then shall ye also with him be manifested in glory."

The reference here clearly is to the future, personal, visible coming of Christ. It is to be an appearing in divine majesty. In all the splendor of that advent his followers are to have a real part. Then their outward state and their moral character are to be made glorious. Their perfected spirits are to be clothed with immortal bodies. They are to share the glory of the ascended, returning Christ. John writes, "When he shall appear, we shall be like him; for we shall see him as he is." (King James Version.)

Paul does not state this truth, however, as a ground for idle speculation or for selfish dreams. Rather, it is the basis for the most practical exhortation to turn from sin and to seek for moral and spiritual progress. The Christ in whom the believer is now "hid," the Christ who is yet to appear in visible glory, is the Christ who must now be "manifested" in the lives of those who bear his name.

V. The Christian Life.   Chs. 3:5 to 4:6

1. THE OLD LIFE AND THE NEW.   Ch. 3:5–17

a. Put Off the Old.   Ch. 3:5–11

5 Put to death therefore your members which are upon the earth: fornication, uncleanness, passion, evil desire, and covetousness, which is idolatry; 6 for which things' sake cometh the wrath of God upon the sons of disobedience: 7 wherein ye also once walked, when ye lived in these things; 8 but now do ye also put them all away: anger, wrath, malice, railing, shameful speaking out of your mouth: 9 lie not one to another; seeing that ye have put off the old man with his doings, 10 and have put on the new man, that is being renewed unto knowledge after the image of him that created him: 11 where there cannot be Greek and Jew, circumcision and uncircumcision, barbarian, Scythian, bondman, freeman; but Christ is all, and in all.

The practical and hortatory section of the epistle consists of two parts, the first containing exhortations relating to the Christian life in general, ch. 3:5–17, and the second containing exhortations concerning various social relations, chs. 3:18 to 4:6.

All these exhortations are based upon the great truths set forth in the earlier portions of the epistle. There Paul has demonstrated the supremacy and sufficiency of Christ in his divine person and his atoning work; he has shown that believers are complete in him and have no need to depend upon religious rites or ascetic practices; by faith they have died with Christ and have risen with Christ to a new and higher life.

In view of these great realities believers are exhorted to put off the sinful passions and habits which characterized the old life and to manifest the virtues which reveal and become the new.   Thus Paul always relates doctrine and duty, creed and character, belief and conduct.   He avoids the folly of those who regard religion as consisting in the acceptance of dogmas, and the error of those who urge high ethical conduct with no basis in Christian belief. According to Paul, the true acceptance of Christ as Lord and Saviour must and will result in a new and a higher life.

"Put to death therefore your members which are upon the earth," writes the apostle. The "therefore" is emphatic. It is the link which unites all the doctrine which precedes with all the exhortations which follow. More specifically it refers to the fact that the believer "died with Christ" and has been "raised . . . with Christ," that he belongs to a heavenly realm and is not to set his mind "on the things that are upon the earth."

Because this is true he must make a supreme effort to slay all evil passions and all sins of temper and speech. These are described by the words, "Your members which are upon the earth." The members of the body, as formerly controlled by sin, are used to picture the various forms of evil which were once practiced and which now must be put to death as belonging not to the new life but to the old. To put these aside is not easy. It is a matter of amputation, of crucifixion. It indicates pain and blood and the agonies of death. It is glorious to be a Christian; it is not easy.

The "members" named form rather a disgraceful list. We might well wish that they had vanished in the first century and need not be named to-day. They all relate to forms of unholy love, just as the other list named in this same paragraph centers in forms of wicked hate. First of all are "fornication," or immorality; then "uncleanness," or impurity in general; and then "passion" and "evil desire," which are sins of thought leading to the two previous classes of sins of action. Thus the series expands from a single sin to the whole range of evil longings.

Last of all Paul mentions "covetousness," which is another form of self-gratification and too often connected with the sins of impurity already named. The word for covetousness used by Paul indicates not only the "lust for gain," but has some implication of taking unfair advantage in the pursuit of profit. It is designated as "idolatry." Anything which is put in the place of God as the supreme object of trust and devotion is an idol. Particularly the pursuit of riches may become a form of religion, and one may worship gold instead of God.

Against all these sins Paul gives his solemn warning. He insists that they call down the judgment of heaven upon those who abandon themselves to them. "For which things' sake," he writes, "cometh the wrath of God upon the sons of disobedience." Those who habitually and continually live in defiance of God, and repudiate their divine origin and destiny, are thus designated as "sons of disobedience." Upon them "cometh the wrath of God." The phrase must not be supposed to indicate anything akin to human passion or malice. The "wrath of God" must be consistent with the love of God. Paul reminds us in Ephesians of the "great love wherewith he loved us, even when we were dead through our trespasses." Yet a holy God must feel and must reveal displeasure with sin. The present consequences of impurity and selfishness are everywhere evident. They are as bitter and terrible as they are familiar, and they are prophetic of more solemn judgments yet to come.

Paul further enforces his exhortation by an appeal to memory: "Wherein ye also once walked, when ye lived in these things." Like the rest of the pagan world the Colossians had once been guilty of these sins. They had practiced them; they had indeed "lived" in them. Their evil conduct had manifested their inclinations and desires. Their daily practice had issued from their inner life.

The memory of that dark past and of their deliverance from its power should impel the readers to renounce and "put to death" the sins Paul has defined, and also to discard those which he proceeds to name. The figure of speech is changed somewhat as he now specifies not forms of impure love but forms and results of unholy hate. He speaks of them as of unclean garments which the pure soul should be eager to cast aside: "But now do ye also put them all away: anger, wrath, malice, railing, shameful speaking out of your mouth: lie not one to another."

In speaking of the former vices Paul declared that the Colossians, as well as other Gentiles, once practiced them: "Wherein ye also once walked." He now insists that they "also," in common with other Christians, should abandon these sins: "Now do ye also put them all away." They have joined a holy brotherhood. Their conduct should conform to that of their new comrades. They should strip themselves of the garments which were the recognized uniform of their former service of sin. They are to "put them all away," all those already named, and all other forms of evil, a few of which he now proceeds to list.

The former catalogue began with acts and moved forward to motives; the present begins with motives and then specifies the actions in which evil emotions result. The former concerned impure affection; these concern lack of love. The former were personal; these are social sins. The former are related to passion, these to speech.

The first to be mentioned are "anger" and "wrath" and "malice." "Anger" is the deep-seated feeling of ill will. "Wrath" is the fiery outburst of temper. "Malice" is settled, cruel malignity, which rejoices in evil to others.

Then follow "railing" and "shameful speaking," which are two expressions of a malicious spirit. The former indicates reckless and bitter abuse; the latter foul language directed against another. Last in the list comes lying, which is made more emphatic by being put in the form of a command: "Lie not one to another." It belongs in this list, for falsehood is usually due to lack of love and is commonly an instrument of malice and hatred.

It might seem unnecessary for Paul to urge such elementary moral conduct upon persons who were declared to be complete in Christ, whose lives were "hid with Christ in God." However, these names of sin specified have a very modern sound. There is something humiliating in the fact that such exhortations are ever needed by Christians to-day. Surely they are in contrast with the professions and possibilities of the Christian life.

This is exactly the thought of the apostle as he states the reason for putting away all these forms of evil. This must and should be done, "seeing that ye have put off the old man with his doings, and have put on the new man, that is being renewed unto knowledge after the image of him that created him."

Again the metaphor is somewhat mixed. The idea is quite clear. When one accepts Christ he puts off his old nature, his old life, with all its deeds. He puts on a new nature, a new life. He professes so to do. Such is ideally his experience. However, in reality it is only the beginning of a process. Much that is evil remains; this must be put aside. On the other hand there are many virtues to be "put on." By a continual process the Christian "is being renewed unto knowledge," the full knowledge which was included in God's gracious purpose when he gave to the believer a new life through faith in Christ. This new life, this new nature, is created in the moral image of God and is to be developed more and more into his likeness.

In this new life distinctions of race and religion and social condition practically cease to exist. Christ occupies the whole sphere. He is all. The holiness, the virtues, the graces, the love which displaces impure desire and destroys enmity, are all from him. "There cannot be Greek and Jew, circumcision and uncircumcision, barbarian, Scythian, bondman, freeman; but Christ is all, and in all."

In the list of surface distinctions which disappear in the new spiritual realm Paul, in Galatians, mentions also "male and female." However, the reader must be guarded against too literal an interpretation, and too general an application of these terms. One must not needlessly defy social customs, or deny legal rights, or offend religious prejudices. In this very chapter Paul distinguishes between wives and husbands, and between servants and masters. These distinctions actually have not ceased; they cannot be ignored. One cannot maintain exactly the same relation with a barbarian and Scythian as with a Christian and a scholar. Marriage is still a sacred institution. However, these racial and national and social distinctions cease to be important to a Christian. They lose their relative significance when Christ becomes supreme. The new nature is not different in differing races and nations. Christian virtues are universal. Those who are being renewed after the image of God have identical needs and common experiences and the same glorious destiny. All men need Christ; all can receive Christ; and all who accept this divine Saviour and Lord partake of the same spiritual life and are one in him.

Belief in such realities does break down and will at last abolish all artificial and accidental barriers between individuals and races and nations and classes. It is this which has already made of the Christian Church a universal brotherhood. It is this which will ultimately solve the stubborn problems of national and social and racial divisions. These must disappear in the perfected Kingdom of God.

b. Put On the New. Ch. 3:12–17

12 Put on therefore, as God's elect, holy and beloved, a heart of compassion, kindness, lowliness, meekness, long-suffering; 13 forbearing one another, and forgiving each other, if any man have a complaint against any; even as the Lord forgave you, so also do ye: 14 and above all these things *put on* love, which is the bond of perfectness. 15 And let the peace of Christ rule in your hearts, to the which also ye were called in one body; and be ye thankful. 16 Let the word of Christ dwell in you richly; in all wisdom teaching and admonishing one another with psalms *and* hymns *and* spiritual songs, singing with grace in your hearts unto God. 17 And whatsoever ye do, in word or in deed, *do* all in the name of the Lord Jesus, giving thanks to God the Father through him.

Christianity is not only negative but also positive. It does not consist in prohibitions and restraints, but it concerns the imparting of a new life and secures continual spiritual progress. Paul has exhorted the Colossians, as those who "died with Christ," to put aside the vices and evil practices of the old life; he now exhorts them, as those who "were raised together with Christ," to put on all the virtues and graces which belong to the new.

"Put on therefore," writes the apostle, "as God's elect, holy and beloved, a heart of compassion, kindness, lowliness, meekness, longsuffering," and to these he then adds forbearance and forgiveness and love.

The word "therefore" links the exhortation to the thought which immediately precedes. "Ye . . . have put on the new man," Paul has reminded his readers, "therefore" they are to "put on" the characteristics which belong to this new nature. They have entered a spiritual sphere in which natural distinctions of race and creed and culture and class have lost their significance, "therefore," they must manifest those virtues which will maintain peace and unity in their new fellowship of faith. The virtues specially enumerated are such as contrast with the last list of vices which were to be "put off," namely, the social sins of ill temper and unkind speech. These virtues, which are to be "put on," are manifestations of love which make for harmony among the followers of Christ.

The basis for the exhortation is expressed in the phrase, "As God's elect, holy and beloved." These terms are all borrowed from the Old Testament. They indicate that the Church is the true Israel; at the same time they imply the experiences which belong to each individual follower of Christ.

All Christians are in a real sense "God's elect." This new life is due, not to any merit of their own, but to the purpose and providence of God. They are "holy and beloved," as those who because of the choice of God have been called into his service and are the objects of his love.

As such, they should be clothed with the virtues which become so lofty a destiny. Among these beautiful garments of the renewed soul the first to be mentioned is pity, or "a heart of compassion." This forms one of the most prominent features in the portrait of Christ as drawn by the Gospel writers. It describes his feeling for the multitudes, for the poor, for the widow, for the blind. It is a sentiment which easily can be stifled by selfishness, by familiarity with distress, and by not being given free expression in action.

"Kindness" is that goodness of heart which enables a man to meet the world with a smile and to act generously toward others, responding with cheerfulness to every call for help. "Lowliness," or humility, was not admired by the ancients but was praised by Christ. It places self last, and so is related to pity and kindness. It regards self as least, and so is related to "meekness" and "long-suffering."

"Meekness" should not suggest anything of weakness or of unreality. It is found in the strongest characters, as in Moses and Christ. The latter described himself as "meek and lowly in heart," and pronounced his beatitude upon the meek: "They shall inherit the earth." Meekness accepts without murmuring whatever God may assign, and without resistance any evil which men may inflict. It is contrasted with harshness or rudeness. "Longsuffering," however, is contrasted with malice, resentment, or revenge. It denotes patience under provocation, self-restraint when tempted to act swiftly or severely.

Paul then adds forbearance and forgiveness: "Forbearing one another, and forgiving each other." The former denotes mutual self-control when two persons are inclined to injure one another. The latter includes the taking out of the heart of all resentment and ill will. The reason for such forgiveness and the supreme example is found in Christ: "Even as the Lord forgave you, so also do ye."

Last of all in his list of heavenly garments Paul mentions "love": "And above all these things put on love, which is the bond of perfectness." "Above all" does not mean most of all, but "over all." Love is pictured as an outer garment, or more exactly, a belt, which not only completes the costume but also perfects and unites all the garments. It is the "bond of perfectness." It binds all the virtues into a harmonious unity, or, as some understand, it binds all Christians into the perfection of a common spiritual life. Both ideas are true, but probably the reference here is not to Christian believers, but to the Christian virtues, each one of which is completed and all of which are fastened together by the girdle of love.

The clothing of the renewed soul is not more important than the conduct of that soul. Thus when Paul has urged his readers to "put on" those virtues which he describes under the figure of garments, he closes this section of his epistle with three exhortations to actions which these virtues should inspire. The first concerns "the peace of Christ," the second, "the word of Christ," the third, "the name of the Lord Jesus."

"The peace of Christ" is named as the ruling principle
which is to guide the life of believers, whether as individuals or as members of the one spiritual body to which
all belong. "Let the peace of Christ rule in your hearts,
to the which also ye were called in one body." "The peace
of Christ" means that peace which Christ imparts. The
deep tranquillity of soul which Christ enjoyed in the midst
of bitter enemies, surrounded by surging crowds, or facing
the cruel cross—such peace he bequeathed to his followers:
"Peace I leave with you; my peace I give unto you." By
such peace his followers should allow their hearts to be
controlled. The Greek word translated "rule" or "arbi-
trate" had originally the meaning of "acting as umpire."
Something of that idea may still be retained. Questions
and problems and courses in life must be determined, not
by passion or in mental turmoil, but as peace determines,
or according to that which makes for peace.

The enjoyment of such controlling tranquillity of heart
was in accordance with the purpose of Christ when he
called us into the Christian life. He intended his peace to
be realized, not only in individual lives, but also in the
unity of his Church. Paul adds, "To the which also ye
were called in one body." If such is the purpose of the
Master for each of his disciples, how eager each should be
to realize in personal experience this gracious design; how
careful also to maintain among the members of the Church
the harmony which becomes a body which is united in
the common possession of this priceless gift!

With something of abruptness Paul adds, "And be ye
thankful," or, more literally, "Become thankful." This
may mean, "Do not fail to be grateful." This virtue must
be cultivated with effort. It well may be called forth by a
remembrance of the goodness of Christ in granting us his
peace.

"Let the word of Christ dwell in you richly." Obedience
to this exhortation would aid in maintaining "the peace
of Christ" concerning which Paul has been speaking. The
exhortation is, however, quite distinct, and is the second
of the three injunctions which are addressed to believers
both as individuals and as members of the Church. "The

word of Christ" means the "word spoken by Christ," or
"the message of Christ." It refers to the teachings of
Christ, or, more specifically, to the gospel, or that whole
body of truth which concerns the person and work of
Christ. This must be allowed to "dwell" in believers.
It should have its home in their hearts and minds. There
it is to be given a permanent abode. Moreover, it is to
dwell there "richly," that is, in all its wealth of meaning
and power, and with all its wide application to every
sphere of life and to every phase of human experience.

Just as in the case of "the peace of Christ," so that
"word of Christ" is for the individual heart; yet it is to
dwell also, and consequently, in the whole body of believers. The result will be that the Church will be more
fully instructed in Christian truth. "In all wisdom teaching and admonishing one another," writes the apostle.
Teaching specially concerns doctrine; admonition concerns
life. If "the word of Christ" is dwelling richly in the body
of believers, they will be able to instruct and guide one
another in every kind of wisdom which concerns Christian
belief and conduct.

The instruction may be given in many ways, as by
example or by speech and conference; but Paul specifies
the occasions of social worship and the particular instrument of sacred song: "Teaching and admonishing one
another with psalms and hymns and spiritual songs." It
may be difficult to distinguish accurately between these
three forms of praise. The first referred probably to the
psalms of the Old Testament, although the application
was not so restricted. It might denote sacred songs composed by the worshipers or expositions of the psalms.
The primary meaning is that of "songs set to music," and
surely no other psalms have been more widely accepted
or more loved than those of The Psalter, which is always
associated with the name of "the sweet psalmist of Israel."

"Hymns" were poems sung in praise of God. Thus
Augustine insisted that "there are three essentials of a
hymn: It must be praise; it must be addressed to God;
it must be sung." It is possible that in Eph. 5:14 and
in I Tim. 3:16 there may be found fragments of early Chris-

tian hymns. It is deeply significant, too, that Pliny, when governor of Bithynia, not many years after the death of Paul, reported to the emperor that the Christians were in the habit of meeting before dawn "to sing a hymn antiphonally to Christ as to a god."

"Songs" was used more widely of many forms of poetry, not only sacred but secular as well. Therefore, the word "spiritual" is added to denote the religious character of these compositions. They were "spiritual," not in the sense of being divinely inspired, but because they were composed by spiritual men and belonged to the sphere of spiritual realities.

It is true that "hymns," the second of these terms, is used properly at the present time to describe all three of these forms of poetical compositions arranged for use in Christian worship. It is probably true that a larger proportion of the religious poems which are used in public praise should be "hymns" in the stricter sense. They should be addressed to God. Too many are subjective, not to say sentimental, and express only personal experiences and aspirations which are sometimes lacking in reality.

It is with something of this thought in mind that Paul adds the words, "Singing with grace in your hearts unto God." In true worship the singing must be not only with the lips; there must be a corresponding song in the heart. In fact, the music must first be in the heart and must continue in the heart. It is this alone which can secure beauty and sincerity.

The singing must be also "with grace." Some prefer to translate this phrase, "With gratitude," or, "With thanksgiving"; but probably it means, "By help of divine grace," or with a conscious dependence upon divine grace.

Above all, true praise must be addressed "unto God." Hymns are not to express merely our happiness or our personal emotions; they must be directed to the Giver of "every perfect gift," to the Author of all spiritual life.

Thus while Paul gives no explicit directions for public worship, he does indicate that in it a large place should be given to sacred song, and that this praise should rise from hearts in which "the word of Christ" is dwelling richly, to which the Spirit of Christ is supplying constant stores of grace.

Paul reaches the climax of his general exhortations by one which is of the widest possible application: "And whatsoever ye do, in word or in deed, do all in the name of the Lord Jesus." Obedience to this command ennobles all life. Not only hymns of praise but every word spoken and every act performed may be transfigured into real worship of God. The one condition is that all shall be done "in the name of the Lord Jesus." This does not mean that this holy name is to be used as a magic charm. A "name" is that by which one is known, or that which one is known to be. The "name of the Lord Jesus" means all that he is or has been revealed to be. What we do in virtue of all that he is to us is real worship. He is our Lord, our Saviour, our Master. Whatever we do trusting his power, obeying his will, or in devotion to his service, is done "in his name." Such a relationship to him gives to all life an abiding gladness, so that Paul can add, "Giving thanks to God the Father through him." Continual gratitude is a duty; continual thanksgiving is a privilege. Our praises and all the service of our lives are accepted as an offering of sweet savor when presented in the name and because of the merits of our Lord Jesus Christ.

2. THE CHRISTIAN HOUSEHOLD. Chs. 3:18 to 4:1

18 Wives, be in subjection to your husbands, as is fitting in the Lord. 19 Husbands, love your wives, and be not bitter against them. 20 Children, obey your parents in all things, for this is well-pleasing in the Lord. 21 Fathers, provoke not your children, that they be not discouraged. 22 Servants, obey in all things them that are your masters according to the flesh; not with eye-service, as men-pleasers, but in singleness of heart, fearing the Lord: 23 whatsoever ye do, work heartily, as unto the Lord, and not unto men; 24 knowing that from the Lord ye shall receive the recompense of the inheritance: ye serve the Lord Christ. 25 For he that doeth wrong shall receive again for the wrong that he hath done: and there is

no respect of persons.   Ch. 4:1 Masters, render unto your servants that which is just and equal; knowing that ye also have a Master in heaven.

Paul paints a charming picture of the Christian home. He does so in a series of exhortations addressed to wives and husbands, to children and parents, to slaves and masters.   It may be noted that Christianity has added no new element to the family.   Hundreds of years before Christ, Aristotle stated that the three great pairs of mutual relations of which family life is constructed are: "husband and wife, parent and child, master and servant."   It is exactly these three relations to which Paul here refers.

It may be noted further that Christianity has proposed no new bond of family life.   In all ages families have been held together by two simple principles, namely, authority and obedience—authority on the part of the husband, the father, the master, and obedience on the part of the wife, the child, the servant.   It is these familiar principles which Paul enjoins his readers to observe.

However, it should be noted that Christianity has introduced into the family a new Presence, even that of the divine Lord.   This Presence has transfigured and glorified every human relationship.   All duties are performed as in his sight.   All life is lived in fellowship with him.   Thus Paul insists that wives are to be in subjection, "as is fitting in the Lord"; children are to obey, "for this is well-pleasing in the Lord"; servants are to obey as "fearing the Lord," and are to "work heartily, as unto the Lord."

The family, like the Church and the State, is a divine institution.   It was not new in the days of Paul.   What was new was the Christian home.   It constitutes one of the richest gifts of Christ to the world.   In it the natural obligations and responsibilities of domestic and social life are not ignored.   They are made only more sacred and more secure.

Thus, when Paul is exhorting wives and husbands, it must be remembered that he is addressing Christians. They are to perform their obligations for the sake of Christ; they are to accept their responsibilities as those who belong to Christ. All human relationships are to be regarded as subordinate to the lordship of Christ.

"Wives, be in subjection to your husbands," writes Paul, "as is fitting in the Lord." It is their Christian duty; it befits Christian women. In such submission there is nothing humiliating or degrading. It is not inconsistent with intellectual and moral and spiritual equality. It is merely the recognition of an authority which is essential to social and domestic order and welfare. It is the natural expression of love which manifests itself in willing service and finds joy in giving pleasure.

Nor is this subjection unlimited. Obviously a wife must not submit when obedience requires an action contrary to conscience, or conduct at variance with the expressed will of God.

Then again there are cases in which because of obviously superior gifts, ability, and faithfulness, the wife assumes the real headship in the home. Such a situation, however, is not ideal. Furthermore, mere listless, thoughtless subjection is not desirable if ever possible. The quick wit, the clear moral discernment, the fine instincts of a wife make of her a counselor whose influence is invaluable and almost unbounded.

However, the real limitation upon the authority of the husband is expressed in the words which follow: "Husbands, love your wives, and be not bitter against them." If not strictly a limitation of authority, perfect love transforms and controls the exercise of authority. It makes tyranny and unkindness, selfishness and cruelty, absolutely impossible. It removes from the submission expected of a wife all that is distasteful or difficult. Indeed it places a husband in a position of actual subjection, for he is compelled by love to obey every claim the wife may make for support, for sympathy, for protection, for happiness. Love is unselfish, patient, self-sacrificing, unfailing. Love makes it impossible for one to be "bitter," that is, harsh, unfeeling. A wife never need fear to obey a husband of whose love she is sure.

Submission on the part of children is likewise required

by the Christian ideal. "Children, obey your parents in all things." No limitation is expressed, and the whole duty of childhood is summed up in the one word "obey." This is the essence of the Fifth Commandment: "Honor thy father and thy mother." To this Commandment the promise is added: "That thy days may be long upon the land which the Lord thy God giveth thee." In Paul's exhortation the ground for obedience is stated in the words, "For this is well-pleasing in the Lord." It is beautiful. It meets the approbation of the Christian community. It accords with Christian standards. It secures the happiness of the Christian home.

On the other hand, parents are to be on their guard lest they be unreasonable and discouraging in their demands. Fathers are specially addressed; not ignoring the authority of mothers, but because fathers have the greater responsibility as the heads of households, and further because they are more apt to be stern and exacting. "Fathers, provoke not your children, that they be not discouraged." The term "provoke" is practically equivalent to "irritate." Unjust and severe treatment and continual faultfinding may result in making a child lose heart and become sullen and listless and depressed.

The last of the domestic duties to be enjoined by the apostle are those of servants and masters. Here the essential requirements are obedience on the part of servants and justice on the part of masters. It is to be noted that these "servants" are not employees but slaves. They are not wage earners, but the actual property of their masters. However, the principles here set forth apply to all servants and to all employers of labor, whether in the household or in the world of industry. If observed they would go far toward solving most of the problems which now threaten the stability of the social order.

The fact that the servants here addressed are "bond-servants" indicates in part the attitude of Paul toward the monster evil of slavery. He does not condemn or attack the system. He does not arouse an insurrection or lead a revolution. He advocates, however, those principles of brotherhood and justice and Christian sympathy by which the roots of the tree finally would be cut and the accursed institution destroyed.

Furthermore, it is evident that when in this epistle Paul declares that in the spiritual realm "there cannot be Greek and Jew, . . . bondman, freeman," he does not mean that Christians should defy all social customs and all civil laws. Slaves were not encouraged to demand freedom. The words of Paul were quite to the contrary: "Servants, obey in all things them that are your masters according to the flesh." They were slaves only as far as human relationships were concerned. In a higher realm they were freemen and equals of their owners. Yet until these higher laws had modified the statutes of society and the regulations of the state, slaves were to recognize the legal rights of their masters and to render to them implicit obedience.

It is significant that this letter to the Colossian church is accompanied by one to Philemon, a Colossian slave owner to whom Paul is sending back a runaway slave. Possibly this may be the reason why the apostle devotes here twice as much space to the relation of slaves and masters as he does to all the other social relations put together.

The obedience, then, of servants is to be not only "in all things," but is to be faithful and loyal and worthy of their Christian profession: "Not with eye-service, as men-pleasers, but in singleness of heart, fearing the Lord." "Eye-service" is such as is rendered only when under close inspection; it makes a false show of industry and a great pretense of diligence. It was a common fault of slaves; in the case of wage earners it is a sin and a crime. Such service might not be detected, and so might please human masters; such slaves might attempt to be "men-pleasers"; but Paul enjoins "singleness of heart," that is, "undivided purpose," aiming only to be faithful to duty and devoted to one's task. The real motive is not to be the desire to please men, but "fearing the Lord," dreading the displeasure of him who is the real Master and Lord.

More positive still is the injunction, "Whatsoever ye do, work heartily, as unto the Lord, and not unto men." Slaves were to labor cheerfully and to put their whole hearts into their work. Even more than that, they were to make of their drudgery and menial toil a sacred and religious duty, as though they were not working for men alone but were working for their divine Lord.

Then Paul adds the great encouragement to such loyal service: "Knowing that from the Lord ye shall receive the recompense of the inheritance." Slaves received no wages upon earth and were allowed no legal right of inheritance; for them, however, there was laid up an inheritance in heaven. They would at last receive from their true Master a just and full reward. There need be no doubt of such a reward, for their real service was not being rendered to human Masters. Their real service was to Christ. Thus Paul adds: "Ye serve the Lord Christ."

In conflicts between employers and employees, between masters and servants, there are often wrongs on both sides. It is not always easy to determine "that which is just and equal." However, much light comes from keeping in mind the principle which Paul states as an encouragement, or a warning, to all masters, as he concludes with the words: "Knowing that ye also have a Master in heaven." Masters are to act toward their servants as they hope their Lord will deal with them. All the kindness, all the sympathy, all the forbearance which they have received from Christ they are to show toward those whose obedience and loyalty they expect. Most of the difficulties in social and industrial life would disappear if "masters" always sought to do what is "just and equal," and if they were ever mindful of the will and the love of their Master in heaven.

3. PRAYERFULNESS AND DISCRETION.   Ch. 4:2-6

2 Continue stedfastly in prayer, watching therein with thanksgiving; 3 withal praying for us also, that God may open unto us a door for the word, to speak the mystery of

Christ, for which I am also in bonds; 4 that I may make it manifest, as I ought to speak. 5 Walk in wisdom toward them that are without, redeeming the time. 6 Let your speech be always with grace, seasoned with salt, that ye may know how ye ought to answer each one.

Paul brings to a climax his practical precepts by exhortations to earnestness in prayer, and to wisdom in action and in speech. "Continue steadfastly in prayer," he writes, meaning that Christians should be careful to maintain special seasons for communion with God, should at all seasons cultivate the consciousness of the presence of God, and, more specifically, should be persistent in their requests to God. They should be like the importunate friend whom the Master described, begging bread at midnight, or like the widow who would not be denied her plea. They are to be "unwearied in prayer."

Moreover, they are to be alert, "watching therein." In the very act of prayer they must be on their guard against wandering thoughts. They must arouse themselves, and beware of indifference and languor. They must concentrate their minds, so that prayer becomes a reality and not an empty form.

Then, too, it must be permeated by a spirit of gratitude, "watching therein with thanksgiving." This latter was a characteristic of the prayers of Paul. Again and again in this very epistle he urges upon his readers the blessed habit of giving thanks. The recognition of the goodness of God inclines one to pray, and helps one to be steadfast and earnest in the practice of prayer.

In the petitions of the Colossians Paul craves a special part. "Withal praying for us also," he writes, probably including in his request the thought of such companions as Timothy and Epaphras. The purpose of the prayer was not to be the comfort or profit of the apostle, but the furtherance of the gospel: "That God may open unto us a door for the word." Paul was in prison. Even there he had found opportunities for proclaiming "the word." In the whole *prætorium*, and indeed throughout the whole city of Rome, the influence of this dauntless messenger of Christ had been felt. Yet he longed to be set free. He

could not address his readers in distant Colossæ without
thinking of the vast spaces he had covered by his missionary journeys, and without yearning to carry out his plans
of preaching Christ in boundless regions yet unreached.
Christ was indeed the sum and essence of his message.
His expressed desire was "to speak the mystery of Christ."

The great revelation of the saving grace of God had
been made manifest in Christ, so that Christ himself was
the Mystery, in the Pauline sense of something once concealed but now revealed.   To one aspect of the gospel
message the word "mystery" may have pointed specially,
namely, to the truth that the gospel message was intended
for Gentiles as well as for Jews, and that Jews and Gentiles
were united in one body through faith in Christ.   Paul
could add truly, "For which I am also in bonds," because
it was specifically his attitude toward the Gentiles that
had resulted in his arrest and his imprisonment.   However, it is quite as true that it was his preaching of Christ
to Jews and Gentiles for which he was in bonds.   This
wider reference is probably what is intended here, for
Paul adds in reference to the whole gospel message as
centering in Christ, "That I may make it manifest, as I
ought to speak."   He wishes for grace to make clear the
deep and hidden mysteries of the gospel and to be given
power of utterance befitting so majestic a theme.   Chafing
under his restraining bonds, and conscious of personal
weakness and imperfection, he makes the request which
every minister of Christ may well repeat to his parishioners
and friends—that he may so be remembered in prayer
that all obstacles may be removed and that he may be
enabled to present with clearness and power the marvelous
message of "the mystery of Christ."

In his concluding exhortation Paul deals with the relation of Christians and unbelievers.   Toward those who are
outside the Church Christians must be wise in their
actions and gracious in their words.   "Walk in wisdom
toward them that are without" is thus an encouragement
to such discreet conduct as will commend and advance
the gospel.   Furthermore, every opportunity of bearing

witness for Christ by kindly act must be eagerly seized. Believers must be ever "redeeming the time." Not only must their lives be consistent, but all their social contacts should be employed for furthering the Christian cause.

However, Christ can be honored not only by conduct but by conversation. "Let your speech be always with grace" is an exhortation to be winsome and pleasing and courteous in one's words. To be such "always" is difficult. It is easy to be affable and gracious on certain occasions, but to speak with sweetness and gentleness when opposed or misrepresented or wronged is a severe test of character; but it is a convincing witness to the power of Christ. Yet Christian conversation, and Christian messages, are not to be insipid and tasteless. They are to be "seasoned with salt." The uses of salt are to give flavor and to prevent corruption. The speech of a Christian should be so "seasoned" with true wisdom that it will be attractive and pointed as well as discreet and pure.

The aim of cultivating such pleasing and wise conversation is "that ye may know how ye ought to answer each one." A Christian should seek, therefore, to speak appropriately to "each one" with whom he comes into contact, adapting his words and his message to the circumstances and character of each inquirer and acquaintance.

Is it not true that such an exhortation to wise conduct, to the full use of passing opportunities, to attractive speech, and to careful replies, indicates that personal conversations with individuals, quite as much as public preaching, must be continually employed by the followers of Christ to win adherents to the Christian cause?

VI. The Companions of the Apostle.   Ch. 4:7-17

1. commendation of his messengers. Ch. 4:7-9

7 All my affairs shall Tychicus make known unto you, the beloved brother and faithful minister and fellow-servant in the Lord: 8 whom I have sent unto you for this very purpose, that ye may know our state, and that he may comfort your hearts; 9 together with Onesimus, the faithful and beloved brother, who is one of you. They shall make known unto you all things that *are done* here.

The names of the friends grouped around that of the apostle form a brilliant galaxy, shining like stars around a central sun. The mere mention of these names in the various epistles of Paul adds to his writings a tone of reality and an element of deep human interest. The letters are made to be not mere theological essays or moral homilies, but vital messages to living men illustrated and embodied in actual life. In no portion of his letters, excepting possibly the last chapter of the Epistle to the Romans, does Paul give a more fascinating list of his companions than in the closing, or "personal," section of this Epistle to the Colossians. This paragraph may be viewed as a portrait gallery of Paul's friends, or as constituting an entertaining volume of missionary biography.

The first names to be mentioned are those of the men who were bearing this epistle to Colossæ from Rome. These are Tychicus and Onesimus. The former had been a close associate of the apostle for a number of years. He is first mentioned as one of the seven companions who accompanied Paul on his Third Missionary Journey as he was returning from Greece to Jerusalem. Tychicus was a native of the province of Asia and probably a citizen of Ephesus. He had been serving Paul during his imprisonment in Rome, and was selected by the apostle to carry to the churches of Asia the epistle addressed to "the Ephesians." As seems probable, that epistle was to be read to the church at Laodicea. Paul therefore takes the occasion to give to this same messenger the letter addressed to the church at Colossæ. In any case both these letters are intrusted by Paul to Tychicus to be conveyed to Asia from Rome. It was a long and perilous journey. Tychicus must cross Italy to the Adriatic and Greece, must sail the Ægean Sea to Miletus, and then penetrate the steep valley of the Lycos to Laodicea and Colossæ. Yet it was a glorious mission. Not only did he gladden the hearts of those early Christians to whom the epistles were addressed, but he started on their long journey across the centuries the precious letters which have brought light and gladness to countless followers of Christ in all ages and lands.

In addition to the letters which he carried, Tychicus was intrusted with verbal messages from Paul to his friends in Colossæ. "All my affairs shall Tychicus make known unto you," writes Paul. He refers to his personal experiences since he has reached Rome, indeed, to the whole story of his arrest and imprisonment, his testimony for Christ in the Imperial City, the opposition of enemies, the aid of his friends, and his impending trial with its possible issue of acquittal or death.

The character of this companion to whom was intrusted so important a mission is sketched in the apostle's own words: "The beloved brother and faithful minister and fellow-servant in the Lord." The term "brother" indicates the relationship of Tychicus to his fellow Christians. With them he belonged to the most exalted and honorable fraternity in all the world, the brotherhood of believers. In this body Tychicus is designated as a "faithful minister." This term does not describe a church officer or official, but denotes a "servant," and indicates the relation which Tychicus has sustained to Paul. He has been his helper, his assistant. He has ministered to Paul, arranging for his comfort, filling his commissions, possibly serving as his scribe. In all these humble tasks he has been "faithful" and has endeared himself to his great leader and friend.

Paul describes him as a "fellow-servant in the Lord."

Both Tychicus and Paul belonged to Christ. Christ had purchased them with his own blood. They were his bond servants, his slaves. Yet such service was ennobling. It denoted high dignity and enduring rewards. In that service Tychicus and Paul stood on an equality. Their tasks differed. Paul was an apostle, a great leader in the Christian Church. Tychicus was merely a helper whose tasks were comparatively menial and obscure. Yet their common relationship to Christ, as his bond servants, made their differences to disappear and their rank to be the same.

The specific task of Tychicus is not mentioned. He bore the letter which would speak for itself. As to his verbal messages, however, Paul further adds, "Whom I have sent unto you for this very purpose, that ye may know our state, and that he may comfort your hearts." To the "state," the condition, the experiences, the prospects of Paul, reference has already been made as Paul alluded to all his "affairs" which Tychicus would "make known." In speaking of bringing "comfort" to their hearts, Paul sounds a new note. The word does not denote "consolation" so much as "encouragement." The Colossians did need to be relieved of anxiety as to the "state" of the beloved and honored apostle; but much more did they need courage to stand against the currents of false philosophy, to oppose the proud teachers of heresy, and to be true to the pure gospel of their divine Lord.

Tychicus himself must have been trusted by Paul as one who was able to give such aid and support to believers in spiritual peril and beset by religious and moral dangers. It was a high compliment that he should be chosen for this difficult task.

That he succeeded in his mission is evident from the fact that these letters reached their destination and were treasured by the churches of Asia. Furthermore, the evidence of fidelity is attested by the facts that at a later time, when Paul had been released from prison, he stated his purpose of sending Tychicus on a most difficult errand to the churches in Crete, and that subsequently, when again imprisoned in Rome, he dispatched Tychicus to Ephesus to take the place of Timothy, who was called by the apostle to Rome to receive his last farewell before his "departure" to receive the martyr's "crown." Tychicus stands out as an illustration of the dignity and the eternal influence of humble toil and of loving tasks faithfully performed in the service of Christ.

The story of Onesimus has all the fascination of fiction and romance. He belonged in Colossæ. He did so literally for he was a slave, and thus the personal property, of Philemon, a wealthy member of the Colossian church. He had robbed his master and escaped from the city, ultimately drifting to Rome. Here by some providence he met with Paul and by him was brought into the experience of a Christian life. He even became very dear to the heart of Paul and proved to be of great service to the imprisoned apostle. However, he belonged to Philemon, and Paul felt that he must be returned to his master. Tychicus is leaving Rome with letters to the Ephesian and Colossian churches. Paul seizes the opportunity of sending Onesimus with Tychicus back to his owner. This he does, giving him a letter to Philemon which has become one of the most precious fragments from the distant past. It contains personal messages concerning the relation of the master and his slave. In addressing the Colossian church, Paul describes a slave's character in terms which, in view of the past, are almost startling, for he speaks of "Onesimus, the faithful and beloved brother, who is one of you." These are the very terms used in the commendation of Tychicus. However, Onesimus is not the equal of Tychicus in Christian service and so is not designated as a "minister" or "fellow-servant." Yet he evidently possessed personal information concerning Paul and the Christian movement in Rome which could supplement the message of Tychicus. Therefore Paul adds, "They shall make known unto you all things that are done here." Thus these two companions of the apostle are dispatched on their historic journey. Henceforth, through all the Christian ages, they are to be known and loved because their names are mentioned in the letters which they are bearing to the distant churches of Asia.

2. GREETINGS FROM FRIENDS. Ch. 4:10-14

10 Aristarchus my fellow-prisoner saluteth you, and Mark, the cousin of Barnabas (touching whom ye received commandments; if he come unto you, receive him), 11 and Jesus that is called Justus, who are of the circumcision: these only *are my* fellow-workers unto the kingdom of God, men that have been a comfort unto me. 12 Epaphras, who is one of you, a servant of Christ Jesus, saluteth you, always striving for you in his prayers, that ye may stand perfect and fully assured in all the will of God. 13 For I bear him witness, that he hath much labor for you, and for them in Laodicea, and for them in Hierapolis. 14 Luke, the beloved physician, and Demas salute you.

Paul next makes mention of three companions who are Jewish converts to Christianity. They have been of great comfort to Paul in his imprisonment, and they are requesting the apostle to send greetings from them to the Christians in Colossæ. The three friends are Aristarchus, Mark, and Justus.

The first of the three does not occupy a large place in the recorded life of Paul. Yet during long periods of time he seems to have been a constant companion. The earliest mention of his name is in connection with the riot at Ephesus where his life was endangered by the mob in the theater. He was a Macedonian whose home was in Thessalonica. He apparently accompanied Paul on his Third Missionary Journey as Paul traveled from Ephesus to Greece and back to Jerusalem. After Paul's arrest, and after his appeal to Cæsar, Aristarchus embarks with Paul on his westward journey, and appears as Paul's companion during his imprisonment in Rome, being mentioned by the apostle as he writes both to Philemon and to the Colossian church. Probably because of his devoted service to the apostle in his confinement Paul designates him as his "fellow-prisoner."

The second of these Jewish Christian comrades, "Mark, the cousin of Barnabas," is a prominent character in the biography of Paul, and best known as the author of the

Second Gospel. He seems to have become acquainted with Paul at the home of his mother in Jerusalem, and he accompanied Paul and Barnabas from Jerusalem to Antioch. From Antioch he started with Paul and Barnabas in the capacity of an attendant on their First Missionary Journey, but deserted them at Perga. Because of this failure Paul refused to take Mark with him on his Second Missionary Journey. This refusal led to the separation of Paul and Barnabas. However, Paul harbored no resentment against Barnabas, and later on came to have such confidence in the fidelity of Mark that he summoned him to Rome to comfort him in his imprisonment shortly before his death.

This restored confidence is expressed in Paul's message to the Colossians: "Touching whom ye received commandments; if he come unto you, receive him." What these commandments were and when sent, cannot be conjectured, unless the meaning is that the commandments were that, as stated, Mark should be cordially received should he visit the Colossian church. The implication is that Mark's early failure may have been known in Colossæ and prejudice against him still may have been felt. In anticipation of a visit, and to express his own affection, Mark unites with Paul in sending to the Colossians his Christian greeting.

As to the third of these Hebrew Christians who unite with Paul in sending salutations to the Colossian church, nothing further is known. Yet this "Jesus that is called Justus" shares with Aristarchus and Mark the high dignity of receiving from Paul the following praise: "These only are my fellow-workers unto the kingdom of God, men that have been a comfort unto me." Of all the Jewish converts in the Imperial City, these three alone were loyal to Paul in his loneliness and his imprisonment. They alone comforted and encouraged him in his efforts to extend throughout the city the good news concerning Christ.

There were others, however, not Jews but Gentiles by birth, who were faithful to the imprisoned apostle, who

cheered his heart and strengthened his hands. Three of
them in particular wished to send their greetings to the
Colossian church. The first of these was Epaphras. His
name would be better known to the readers of the epistle
than any which had appeared, for Epaphras was a Colossian, and indeed the founder of the church in that city.
It is even probable that, as the delegate and representative of the apostle, he also had established Christianity in
the neighboring cities of Hierapolis and Laodicea. This
had been done during the long stay of Paul in Ephesus.
Many years have passed. Paul is now in Rome, and
Epaphras has arrived with disturbing tidings from Colossæ. He reports the peril in which the Christians of the
region are placed by subtle forms of heresy. To meet this
need Paul writes the epistle. Thus to Epaphras is due
not only the founding of the church but the composition
of the letter. He is not ready to leave Paul. Thus Tychicus is chosen to bear the epistle to Colossæ. However,
Epaphras is eager to send his greeting: "Epaphras, who
is one of you, a servant of Christ Jesus, saluteth you."

A "servant," literally, a slave, or a "bondservant," is a
term frequently applied by Paul to himself. It denotes
the service of absolute devotion to Christ as Master and
Lord. The particular service which Epaphras now is rendering is not that of lowly ministry like that of Tychicus
or Aristarchus, nor that of founding churches or encouraging believers. It is the service of intercessory prayer.
"Always striving for you in his prayers," writes Paul.
The Greek word for "striving" had lost its original meaning of "agonizing," but it still indicated intense mental
concentration and earnest spiritual effort. Such was the
spirit in which Epaphras was praying.

The aim or purpose of his prayer is that the Colossians
"may stand perfect and fully assured in all the will of
God." He would have them stand firm against all the
currents of false belief which threaten to bear them away
from Christ. He would have them be "perfect," increasingly realizing that ideal which Christ revealed and which
he enables believers to attain. He wishes that they may

be "fully assured," convicted and convinced, of all that "the will of God" may be for them.

This eager prayer on the part of Epaphras is due to his deep concern for the Colossians, and also for their Christian brethren in the other cities of the Lycos Valley. "For I bear him witness," is the emphatic statement of the apostle, "that he hath much labor for you, and for them in Laodicea and for them in Hierapolis." It is a beautiful picture which Paul paints of this Colossian pastor bowing his knees in the Roman prison and pleading with God for the spiritual welfare of his flock imperiled by false beliefs in their remote dwelling places in distant Asia.

The last of Paul's companions to send their greetings are Luke and Demas. "Luke, the beloved physician, and Demas salute you"—two men whose memories are strikingly contrasted. One is the very embodiment of fidelity; the other has become a synonym for disloyalty if not disgrace. Luke was a Greek, a man of refinement and culture and of wide and tender sympathies. He is known as the author of the Third Gospel, "the most beautiful book in the world," and also of The Acts. He is best loved, however, for his devotion to Paul. He was with him on at least portions of his Second and Third Missionary Journeys, on his perilous voyage to Rome, and now as the Colossian letter is being written he is sharing imprisonment with Paul. At a later imprisonment he seems to be the sole companion and solace of the apostle, for Paul writes in his last letter, the Second Epistle to Timothy, "Only Luke is with me." In that same letter there occurs the contrasting phrase, "Demas forsook me, having loved this present world." As to this Demas, conjecture has been busy. Excepting these references nothing more of him is known. The language of Paul does not denote absolute apostasy from Christ and possibly nothing more than the desertion of a friend in a time of pitiful need. At the very least it may be noted that his name lost the luster which forever radiates from the honored name of Luke.

3. PERSONAL MESSAGES.   Ch. 4:15-17

15 Salute the brethren that are in Laodicea, and Nymphas, and the church that is in their house. 16 And when this epistle hath been read among you, cause that it be read also in the church of the Laodiceans; and that ye also read the epistle from Laodicea. 17 And say to Archippus, Take heed to the ministry which thou hast received in the Lord, that thou fulfil it.

A personal paragraph brings the epistle toward its close. It includes a salutation from Paul to the Christian brethren in Laodicea, to Nymphas, and to "the church that is in their house."   Then instructions are given as to the use of Paul's letters, and finally a warning to Archippus. Laodicea was only twelve miles from Colossæ, down the valley of the Lycos, and it was natural that Paul should send his fraternal greetings to the Christians resident there.   The exact meaning of the words is not easily determined.   It would seem that Paul is sending his salutation to a particular group meeting in the homes of Nymphas and his family, in addition to the general body of believers in Laodicea.   Separate buildings for Christian worship do not seem to have been in use earlier than the third century.   "The church" in the house of any particular person or persons apparently indicated the circle of Christians accustomed to assemble in that house for worship.   In the larger cities, as Rome, Rom. 16:5, or Ephesus, I Cor. 16:19, there may have been a number of such local congregations in private homes.

Paul next refers to the public reading of his epistles for the edification of the Christian assemblies.   "When this epistle hath been read among you, cause that it be read also in the church of the Laodiceans; and that ye also read the epistle from Laodicea."   The latter of these two letters is quite commonly believed to be identical with what is known as the Epistle to the Ephesians.   This seems to have been an encyclical letter intended by Paul for all the churches of Asia.   As the letter reached Ephesus first, since that was the chief city of Asia, it would be natural for the name of Ephesus to become attached in later years to this epistle.

The public reading of these letters, and the other letters of Paul, and their exchange between the churches, must have deepened the sense of their weight and value for the whole Church of Christ. Indeed, it indicates, in a sense, the origin of the New Testament and the custom of placing these apostolic writings on an equality with all inspired Scripture and reading them in all the assemblies of the Christian churches.

The message "to Archippus" is commonly interpreted quite to the discredit of this Christian worker. "And say to Archippus, Take heed to the ministry which thou hast received in the Lord, that thou fulfil it." This is supposed to imply a rebuke for negligence, or at least a warning against indifference. It may be, however, only a message of encouragement. Unless Archippus was grossly unfaithful, it is impossible that Paul would have administered his censure so publicly and at the close of such an epistle. Archippus is not addressed. The message is to reach him through the Colossian friends. Probably he was not in Colossæ. As the message is combined with two others relating to Laodicea, he may have been in the latter city. The mention of his name as it appears in the address of the letter to Philemon has led to the conjecture that he was a son of Philemon and Apphia. His ministry was probably that of an "evangelist." Therefore without accusing him of being guilty of the lukewarmness which is associated in the Apocalypse with the Laodicean church, Archippus may be regarded as one laboring at Laodicea who is here encouraged to persevere in his difficult task. The message is to reach him through the Colossian church, the church from which he probably received his commission. However, this commission had come ultimately from Christ. It must be discharged, therefore, with the fidelity due to a divine Master. Every opportunity must be improved; every responsibility must be accepted. His is a ministry which must be discharged with absolute fidelity. Such, too, is the "ministry" assigned by Christ to any one of his followers. Whatever the varying spheres of labor, to each one, without any implication of negligence, the exhortation may be addressed: "Take heed to . . . [thy] ministry . . . that thou fulfil it."

VII. The Conclusion. Ch. 4:18

18 The salutation of me Paul with mine own hand. Remember my bonds.   Grace be with you.

Paul dictated his epistles.   His letter to Philemon is apparently the only one written by his own hand.   He did not necessarily employ a professional scribe or secretary. Probably some qualified friend or helper served as his amanuensis.   However, he usually wrote a closing salutation or signature, much as is the custom in signing letters to-day.   Thus in closing the letter to the Colossians he takes the pen into his own hand and writes, "The salutation of me Paul with mine own hand," which is in other words: "Here is my own personal greeting, addressed to the friends to whom I have dictated this letter, together with greetings from their friends.   It is written in my own handwriting and is signed with my own name, Paul." Such signatures gave evidence that the letters were genuine.   Furthermore, they imparted to each a personal touch.   One can imagine the value added to a piece of parchment on which a message was concluded by the autograph of Paul.

As Paul stretches out his hand to grasp the pen, it is imagined that he felt his arm impeded by the chain which bound him to his Roman guard, and that for this reason he is reminded of his wearisome confinement and therefore adds, "Remember my bonds."

Whether Paul himself ever forgot his confinement or not, surely this reminder given to his friends must have awakened sympathy in the hearts of his readers.   Further it must have encouraged them to endure hardship for the cause of Christ should the necessity arise.   Still further, it must be regarded as a claim to authority based on suffering as a servant of Christ.   It is in this last respect like the stern appeal in the close of the Galatian Epistle: "Henceforth let no man trouble me [let none dispute my apostolic authority]; for I bear branded on my body the marks of Jesus."

This reference to his "bonds" must have caused the hearers to regard with a deeper reverence the message which thus concludes, to heed more earnestly his request for their prayers, and to defend more loyally the gospel for which the apostle was sacrificing his life.

The epistle closes with a prayer: "Grace be with you." In this, or in some expanded form, the apostolic benediction concludes all the letters of Paul. It is a petition for "grace." All possible blessings are infolded in that one word. It includes all the unmerited favor and boundless love of God, revealed in Christ and securing for believers peace and power and fullness of life. This grace is needed that those who read this epistle may comprehend the preëminence of Christ, the divine glory of his person and work, and the sufficiency and completeness of all who put their trust in him.

THE EPISTLE OF PAUL
TO PHILEMON

INTRODUCTION

The Epistle to Philemon is commonly regarded as a mere pendant to the Epistle to the Colossians. Both were written by the same author, and at the same time, and dispatched by the same messengers to Colossæ. Philemon was addressed to an individual member of the church, relative to a matter of merely personal concern. Nevertheless, this brief letter has a distinct character of its own and is a priceless gem by which the New Testament is immeasurably enriched.

Philemon was a wealthy householder of Colossæ who had been brought to Christ by the influence of Paul and had begun to use his wealth for the advancement of the Christian cause. This had been during the long stay of Paul in Ephesus. There Philemon had met the apostle, or in his Colossian home had been reached by some messenger of the apostle. Years had passed. Paul had been taken as a prisoner to Rome. By some kind providence Onesimus, a fugitive slave, who had robbed his master, Philemon, and had drifted to Rome, had met with Paul and had been persuaded by him to begin a Christian life. His character was transformed and he became of great service to the apostle in his confinement, winning his confidence and his love. However, Paul was unwilling to retain Onesimus in Rome without the knowledge and consent of his master. An occasion offered for his return to Colossæ. Word reached Paul of serious doctrinal difficulties in the Colossian church. To meet these false teachings he composed a letter which he dispatched by the hand of his friend Tychicus. At the same time he wrote a letter to Philemon in reference to Onesimus, whom he sent with Tychicus back to Colossæ. He pleaded with the master to pardon the returning slave and even to receive him as a brother in Christ. The epistle is, there-

117

fore, unique among the New Testament writings in that it is concerned with a purely private affair. It contains no statement of Christian doctrine, no exhortation to Christian life. However, its value consists in the fact that it offers an object lesson in applied Christianity. It reveals the heart of the great apostle; it demonstrates the power of Christian truth; it furnishes an inspiring example of Christian conduct.

First of all this letter is a model of Christian courtesy. The task which confronted Paul was one of peculiar delicacy. He must compose a message which would win the favor of Philemon yet would not offend Onesimus. He must bring no compulsion to bear upon one who was himself deeply indebted to Paul; he must plead the merits without denying the guilt of one who had been at serious fault. The successful accomplishment of so difficult a task reveals the apostle as an ideal Christian gentleman. Philemon must have been moved by the complimentary references to himself and by the tone and charm of the letter, while Onesimus must have regarded the expressions of Paul's confidence and love as more precious than the pardon and possible freedom which Philemon might bestow.

Paul claims no right to command. He rather pleads as an aged prisoner, making a humble request of one whose generosity and faith he highly commends. He addresses Philemon as his "beloved and fellow-worker." He calls to mind the kindly relief which has been extended by Philemon to members of the Colossian church. He indicates that he is to intercede for one who has been brought by him into fellowship with Christ. It is only after this extended and tender introduction that the name of Onesimus is introduced. The guilty slave is described merely as having been "unprofitable," and as being now Paul's "very heart." It is intimated that his help is invaluable, but that he is being returned lest his service to the apostle may seem to be a taking by compulsion of that which the master would willingly offer. The very hand of God is recognized in the temporary loss of a slave who may now be received in the abiding relationship of a Christian brother. At last Paul comes to the point and makes the request for which the letter is composed. On the ground of Christian fellowship Philemon is asked to receive Onesimus as he would receive Paul. As for any debt or damage, that is to be put to the account of the apostle, who promises to repay, although mindful of the greater debt which Philemon owes him. He expresses confidence that the request will be granted and intimates that he hopes shortly to be released and himself enjoy the hospitality of his friend.

No letter possibly could be more courteous, more tactful, more delicate in its expression. Literature contains other examples of letters which have become famous for their politeness. Among these one most frequently quoted is from the pen of the younger Pliny, a Roman gentleman, a provincial governor, who was born about the year in which the letter to Philemon was written. It is remarkable that he was writing also in reference to a fugitive slave for whose pardon and kindly reception he made his plea. It is the twenty-first in the ninth book of Pliny's letters, and has been translated as follows:

C. Plinius to his friend Sabinianus, Greeting.

Your freedman, with whom you had told me you were vexed, came to me and, throwing himself down before me, clung to my feet, as if they had been yours. He was profuse in his tears and his entreaties; he was profuse also in his silence. In short, he convinced me of his penitence. I believe that he is, indeed, a reformed character, because he feels that he has done wrong. You are angry, I know; and you have reason to be angry, this also I know; but mercy wins the highest praise just when there is the most righteous cause for anger. You loved the man, and I hope you will continue to love him; meanwhile, it is enough that you should allow yourself to yield to his prayers. You may be angry again, if he deserves it; and in this you will be more readily pardoned if you yield now. Concede something to his youth, something to his tears, something to your own indulgent disposition. Do not torture him, lest you torture yourself at the same time. For it is torture to you when one of your gentle temper is angry. I am afraid lest I should appear not to ask, but to compel, if I should add my prayers to his. Yet I will add them the more fully and unreservedly, because I scolded the man myself with sharpness and severity; for I threatened him straitly that I would never ask you again. This I said to him, for it was necessary to alarm him; but I do not use the same language to you. For, perchance, I shall ask again and shall be successful again; only let my request be such as it becomes me to prefer, and you to grant. Farewell!

This letter is indeed graceful and admirable. No wonder that it is commonly known as "The Polite Epistle." However, it is probably safe to affirm that in comparison Paul's Epistle to Philemon is superior in delicacy, in beauty, in warmth. It appears more natural and more spontaneous. There is not the least affectation, nor self-consciousness, nor flattery, nor striving for effect. It is an embodiment of absolute sincerity and perfect courtesy.

Thus it furnishes the pattern which all Christians should follow in the writing of letters. Correspondence forms, for many people, a significant part of the daily task. Letters are more brief than in a past generation, but far more numerous. Courtesy demands that they should be answered promptly, legibly, and with due consideration for the person addressed. It is easy, in this matter, to cause offense. On the other hand, even a brief message may be so phrased as to cause satisfaction and delight.

Courtesy, however, should characterize all the conduct of life. It should be manifest in all the daily contacts with servants and associates, with strangers and friends. It should be the distinguishing feature of one who professes to follow in the footsteps of Christ.

In the second place the Epistle to Philemon is a manifestation of Christian love. In the case of Paul it is evident that the source of his courtesy was to be traced to his kindness of heart. Politeness cannot be taught by books of etiquette, but only by the tuition of love. It is true that no Christian should be willing to offend by ignorance or defiance of social conventions or customs. However, courtesy is inspired by an unselfish consideration for the feelings and happiness of others. It is the fair flower of Christian charity. This spirit breathes through every sentence addressed to Philemon. The epistle abounds in expressions of tender affection. Paul declares his love, not only for the wealthy and generous householder, but also for the fugitive slave. He describes the latter as one who is "profitable," as "a brother beloved," as Paul's "very heart."

This recognition of brotherhood, this declaration of spiritual equality, was destined to undermine and destroy the very institution of slavery, which has been regarded as the greatest curse of society. It was in the days of Paul the "sum of all villanies." A slave was a mere chattel, absolutely without rights. He could be tortured or killed at the caprice of his master. It is reported that a leading Roman was accustomed to cast any offending slave into a pool where the victim was eaten by electric eels kept for the purpose. When in the presence of Augustus a slave of this owner had broken a crystal goblet the command was given that he should be cast to the eels. He fell at the feet of the emperor, begging not for his life but for a more merciful form of death. It is to the credit of Augustus that he secured the release of the slave.

If, then, slavery was such an iniquity why was it tolerated by Paul? Why did he not cry out against it? How was it possible that he was now returning to his master a fugitive who had escaped from bondage? The answer is that Christianity has overcome social evils, not by armed force, not by insurrection, not by violence and revolution, but by the establishment of principles by which institutions of cruelty and inhumanity have been undermined and overthrown. The relation into which Christian faith brought Paul and Onesimus, the relation which Paul was establishing between Onesimus and Philemon by this letter, was destined to make impossible the continued reign of this monstrous system of tyranny and crime which slavery upheld. Thus this little letter to Philemon has been called "The *Magna Charta* of Liberty."

The same is true of the Christian attitude toward war. While every effort should be made to abolish this horror by conferences and limitations of armaments, by covenants

and leagues, wars will never cease until the hearts and
minds of men are controlled by the principles and the
Spirit of Christ. Envy and jealousy, hatred and lust for
power, still imperil the peace of the world. Abiding peace
can be insured only under the reign of love.

Furthermore, this Epistle to Philemon is a monument
of Christian conversion. It demonstrates the fact that
Christ does have the power to transform lives, to cast out
evil, and to redeem and save. It shows that spiritual
rebirth is possible, and that the hearts and minds of men
can be changed and brought under the dominance of
unselfish love. The evils of society can be abolished only
when the individual members of society are brought into
obedience to Christ.

Such is the truth made manifest by the story of Onesimus.
His conversion was surprising, sudden, sincere. It would
be difficult to imagine a more hopeless vagabond than this
Phrygian slave; yet he was transformed into a comrade
and beloved helper of the chief Christian apostle. The
change must have been rapid, for it was due to the influence of Paul while he was a prisoner in Rome; yet the
entire length of Paul's imprisonment was not more than
two years, a considerable portion of which remained when
the epistle was written.

It must have been a sincere conversion, for Onesimus
was facing voluntarily the fate of a runaway slave. He
might expect any indignity, even the agony of the cross.
Yet he was willing to return to the master whom he had
wronged and to submit to any penalty which might be
imposed. Surely Onesimus was a transformed man; his
name has become a symbol of the redeeming power of
Christ.

Did the letter accomplish its purpose? Did Philemon
pardon his offending slave? History contains no answer.
It is difficult to imagine, however, that a request so
exquisitely phrased by the great apostle could have been
refused by his Christian friend. We might even accept

the tradition that Onesimus was set free to return to Rome and to minister to the needs of Paul.

It is easy to understand how readers of the letter have loved to find in the petition of the apostle a faint parallel to the intercession of the Saviour, who paid the debt for his followers, who transforms them by his love and imparts to them something of that true courtesy which characterizes this letter and makes it one of the most charming fragments of the past.

THE OUTLINE

1. THE SALUTATION.   Philemon 1–3

1 Paul, a prisoner of Christ Jesus, and Timothy our brother, to Philemon our beloved and fellow-worker, 2 and to Apphia our sister, and to Archippus our fellow-soldier, and to the church in thy house: 3 Grace to you and peace from God our Father and the Lord Jesus Christ.

According to the custom of the day Paul began his letters with the mention of his own name. It is that name which gives these letters their priceless value, for among the followers of Christ none played a more significant part than did Paul, none wrote more decisively as to Christian faith and life. To his name Paul usually added some descriptive title, indicating his authority. Quite commonly he designated himself "an apostle of Christ Jesus." In addressing Philemon, however, he is to make a request. He is to give no exhortation, no instruction. Therefore, with extreme delicacy, he uses a term which may appeal to the heart of his reader. He calls himself "a prisoner." Such indeed he was, and for long months he had been confined in Rome. To the mind of Philemon the very suggestion must have presented a contrast to the Paul he had known in Ephesus—the Paul of ceaseless activity, the flaming evangelist, the tireless traveler, the unresting administrator and missionary. The intimation that he was now in confinement and bound by chains must appeal at once to the sympathy of his friend.

The term, however, was not one of mere humility. There was about it something of dignity, if not indeed of authority, for Paul adds the name of the divine Lord in whose service his imprisonment is being endured. He designates himself "a prisoner . . . of Christ Jesus." Any request, therefore, which may be made, and any favor which may be granted will be in relation to the cause of the Master to whom both Paul and Philemon belonged. The appeal which follows will thus be enforced by the sympathy and reverence due to one who is suffering for the sake of Christ.

With his own name Paul unites that of Timothy. The latter was the most intimate and beloved friend of the apostle. He was a man of gentle and affectionate disposition, somewhat timid and diffident, yet so loyal and devoted as to be regarded and treated by the apostle as his own son. Why his name is here introduced can only be conjectured. Possibly it was because Timothy had met Philemon in Ephesus or had visited his home in Colossæ. Possibly it indicated that Paul had conferred with Timothy in reference to the return of Onesimus, and thus gave this added testimony to the reality of the conversion of Onesimus and the sincerity of his purpose.

Timothy is called "our brother," referring to the great fraternity of Christian believers to which both Paul and Philemon belonged. Upon this very spirit of brotherhood, engendered by faith in Christ, Paul is depending as he asks that a kindly reception be given to the fugitive slave. This spirit ultimately is destined to abolish the very institution of slavery and to end all similar social wrongs.

The correspondent whom Paul addressed was Philemon. He resided in Colossæ and was the master of Onesimus. From the verses which follow it is evident that he was a Christian whose conversion had been due to the personal influence of the apostle. He was, moreover, a man of wealth and of social position, whose generosity and charity were known throughout the Colossian church. Paul designates him as "our beloved and fellow-worker," which is in effect, "our dear friend and fellow worker." They may possibly have labored together in Ephesus. More probably the words indicate that in the view of Paul the work for Christ being done in the remote city of Colossæ by Philemon was part of the great task being done by Paul in Rome and in all the spheres of his earlier ministry. Thus it is that all who serve Christ are companions in labor. Obscurity and prominence are relative terms and lose all significance when each one strives in his own place and time to perform the task assigned and to seek to please the one divine Master and Lord.

There can be little doubt that "Apphia our sister," or

"Apphia our fellow Christian," to whom Paul sends his greeting, was the wife of Philemon. The prominent place given to her name and the social equality with Philemon and with Paul which the terms intimate remind us of what Christianity has done for womanhood. This is the power to which in largest measure can be traced the emancipation and elevation by which the wife has been placed on a social and spiritual equality with the husband in the ennobling companionship of the Christian home.

The name Archippus is added to those of Philemon and Apphia. He evidently belonged to their household and may have been their son. To him a special message was addressed in the Epistle to the Colossians, a message often interpreted as a rebuke. It was probably merely an encouragement to fidelity: "Say to Archippus, Take heed to the ministry which thou hast received in the Lord, that thou fulfil it." Here he is designated not as a fellow minister, or a fellow worker, but as Paul's "fellow-soldier." This is surely a gracious compliment, and recognizes Archippus as actively engaged with Paul in aggressive, self-denying, Christian service.

The salutation is addressed, further, "To the church in thy house." This may refer to the servants or other members of the household. More probably it meant a group of Christians who were accustomed to assemble in the home of Philemon for worship. Indeed this reference to a Christian circle is significant. It indicates that while the letter which follows is personal and private, nevertheless its contents are of importance both to the family of Philemon and also to the Christian friends with whom he is most intimate. All will be interested in the return of Onesimus. All will need the commendation of the apostle in order that they may be willing to receive a fugitive slave as a Christian brother.

This reference may further indicate the social standing of Philemon, whose home was capable of entertaining a Christian congregation for its seasons of worship. There is a still more important conjecture. This address, "To the church," probably saved the letter from the fate of most personal notes, which are hidden and lost, and led to its being kept by the Christian community and thus brought across the centuries to enrich and instruct Christians in all lands.

The actual greeting is in the form which is familiar in the letters of Paul: "Grace to you and peace from God our Father and the Lord Jesus Christ." It may be regarded as a wish, a prayer, or a promise. It expresses the greatest good one may desire for another. It requests that such good may be granted. It is an assurance that such good will come, for it is sought from a loving God. "Grace" is unmerited favor. It indicates the Source from which all true blessings flow. It indicates, further, not only the Giver, but also the gift. It denotes all that divine bestowal whereby spiritual life is experienced and its needs supplied.

"Peace" is rather the result and the issue of the granting of these gifts. It denotes a right relation with God and with men and, further, the rest and tranquillity of soul which is man's greatest need and highest desire.

These great blessings are expected and assured for they are to come "from God our Father and the Lord Jesus Christ." The form of the reference is such as to leave no doubt that to the mind of the apostle the Father and the Son are one in a divine, unique unity. Looking to this Source every believer may be assured of limitless supplies of "grace" and the enjoyment of a "peace" that passes all understanding.

2. THE THANKSGIVING AND PRAYER. Philemon 4–7

4 I thank my God always, making mention of thee in my prayers, 5 hearing of thy love, and of the faith which thou hast toward the Lord Jesus, and toward all the saints; 6 that the fellowship of thy faith may become effectual, in the knowledge of every good thing which is in you, unto Christ. 7 For I had much joy and comfort in thy love, because the hearts of the saints have been refreshed through thee, brother.

As is usual Paul follows his salutation with a thanksgiving and a prayer. Here, as frequently, these are interwoven. The thanksgiving is expressed in his prayer and is the occasion of his prayer. It precedes and follows his petition. This should ever be the practice and experience of Christians. Gratitude and praise should be the very spirit of intercession.

Paul is grateful for the reports which have been brought to him of the love which Philemon has been showing toward his fellow believers and the faith in Christ which is the source of this love. He expresses this gratitude every time he remembers Philemon in prayer. Thus he declares, "I thank my God always, making mention of thee in my prayers, hearing of thy love, and of the faith which thou hast toward the Lord Jesus, and toward all the saints."

The love of Philemon, therefore, was no mere sentiment, no weak emotion, no empty profession. It was expressed in deeds. It resulted in generous gifts to his fellow Christians. These recipients were called "saints." This was the usual word for Christians. The term originally meant persons who were "set apart," or "consecrated" to the service of God. Then it denoted the holy character naturally associated with such consecration. Even though used commonly by Paul as a familiar designation of believers, something of its original meaning is retained. At least it implies what every Christian should be, in conscious dedication to God and in a life and character corresponding to so high a calling and dignity. Philemon was showing his right to such a name by his deeds of charity and love, and for this Paul was filled with gratitude to God.

His expression of gratitude, however, is combined with a petition for Philemon. Paul prays, "That the fellowship of thy faith may become effectual, in the knowledge of every good thing which is in you, unto Christ." The "fellowship" of Philemon's faith meant that charity and love which his faith in Christ has inspired. Paul prays that it may have a practical effect, namely, that it may lead to a fuller knowledge of Christian life and of the effects of Christian faith, and to a more perfect understanding of the real nature of Christian graces; that all this may be "unto Christ," or may result in the glory of Christ.

As a ground for his assurance in prayer and as a further expression of his thanksgiving Paul adds, "For I had much joy and comfort in thy love, because the hearts of the saints have been refreshed through thee, brother." This expression of happiness and encouragement occasioned by the reported kindness of Philemon forms an admirable introduction to the request which immediately follows and which forms the main body of the letter; for, if Philemon has been so kind and generous, surely he will be glad to show one further deed of Christian love.

3. THE REQUEST.   Philemon 8–22

8 Wherefore, though I have all boldness in Christ to enjoin thee that which is befitting, 9 yet for love's sake I rather beseech, being such a one as Paul the aged, and now a prisoner also of Christ Jesus: 10 I beseech thee for my child, whom I have begotten in my bonds, Onesimus, 11 who once was unprofitable to thee, but now is profitable to thee and to me: 12 whom I have sent back to thee in his own person, that is, my very heart: 13 whom I would fain have kept with me, that in thy behalf he might minister unto me in the bonds of the gospel: 14 but without thy mind I would do nothing; that thy goodness should not be as of necessity, but of free will.   15 For perhaps he was therefore parted *from thee* for a season, that thou shouldest have him for ever; 16 no longer as a servant, but more than a servant, a brother beloved, specially to me, but how much rather to thee, both in the flesh and in the Lord.   17 If then thou countest me a partner, receive him as myself.   18 But if he hath wronged thee at all, or oweth *thee* aught, put that to mine account; 19 I Paul write it with mine own hand, I will repay it: that I say not unto thee that thou owest to me even thine own self besides.   20 Yea, brother, let me have joy of thee in the Lord: refresh my heart in Christ.

21 Having confidence in thine obedience I write unto thee, knowing that thou wilt do even beyond what I say.   22 But withal prepare me also a lodging: for I hope that through your prayers I shall be granted unto you.

Nothing could be more charming, more delicate, more

original than the way in which Paul here pleads for a kindly reception to be given by Philemon to his runaway slave, Onesimus.

Paul begins by intimating that possibly he has a right to command a course of action which, out of love for Philemon, he will only, and humbly, request. "Wherefore," he writes, referring to the charity which has ever characterized the conduct of Philemon and upon which he can now rely, "though I have all boldness in Christ to enjoin thee that which is befitting, yet for love's sake I rather beseech." By "all boldness" Paul means "ample ground for a claim." This ground is that of his apostolic authority. As an apostle directly commissioned by Christ, he might have ordered Philemon to do "that which is befitting," or that which Paul regards as a Christian duty.

However, out of loving consideration for his friend he has chosen rather to implore and to "beseech"; he enforces his request by an appeal not only to affection but to sympathy, if indeed not to actual pity, as he writes, "I . . . beseech, being such a one as Paul the aged, and now a prisoner also of Christ Jesus."

Since Paul was "a young man" at the martyrdom of Stephen, he could not now have been very far advanced in years. Surely he was not over sixty years of age. Yet his sufferings, his anxieties, his incessant labors had made him old before his time. He probably looked and felt as he here describes himself, "Paul the aged."

He adds, however, another phrase, which may make its further appeal to the heart of Philemon, for he describes himself as "a prisoner . . . of Christ Jesus." He has begun the letter with this phrase. Here again he refers to that irksome, cruel confinement which he is enduring. However, he is enduring it for the sake of Christ Jesus. All his pain and distress are being suffered to advance the cause of his Master. Can Philemon refuse a request made by one who is bearing so much for the sake of the Master to whom they both belong?

Only after so long and affecting a prelude does Paul describe the subject of his appeal. Even in mentioning the name he introduces it by two tender phrases: "I beseech thee for my child, whom I have begotten in my bonds, Onesimus." This "brand plucked out of the burning" was specially dear to the apostle because rescued by the apostle while himself a prisoner. Onesimus was "the child of his sorrows." His presence, his spiritual birth, and his rapid development had been to the apostle a chief source of his solace.

If, therefore, he was so precious to Paul, must he not be worthy of consideration and kindness on the part of Philemon? To produce the impression must have been the purpose of holding back the name to this unusual place in the sentence. At last the word is written, "Onesimus." Well did Paul anticipate the reaction which the name would produce in the mind of Philemon—the name of a worthless, criminal, Phrygian slave. Thus at once he diverts the thought and counteracts the effect by an affectionate play upon the name. "Onesimus, did I say? Onesimus means 'helpful,' 'gainful.' Full well do I know that he once was unprofitable to thee, but now is profitable to thee and me."

Even yet Paul does not state his request. He delays it for a much later line, v. 17. He paves the way, however, by stating that he has sent Onesimus back and by describing his conversion and complete change of character. "Whom I have sent back to thee in his own person," writes Paul, "that is, my very heart." Onesimus, the vagabond slave, has become so precious to the apostle that sending him away is like tearing the heart out of his own breast. How sudden and complete a change does this imply! How the words must have astonished Philemon and prepared him for the request!

However, Paul still delays making the request. He states his half-formed purpose to keep Onesimus in Rome: "Whom I would fain have kept with me, that in thy behalf he might minister unto me in the bonds of the gospel." Thus Paul intimates that if Philemon had known all the facts he would gladly have allowed his slave to remain in Rome and to render service to Paul as a representative of his master. However, Onesimus belongs to Philemon. Paul cannot continue to be served by a fugitive slave without the master's knowledge and consent. Therefore, Paul is returning him to Philemon. He has been of real help to Paul in his gospel ministry, or, as here stated, "in the bonds of the gospel," that is, in the imprisonment Paul has incurred in preaching the gospel.

"But without thy mind I would do nothing," writes the apostle; "that thy goodness should not be as of necessity, but of free will." By his "goodness" Paul meant the kindness of Philemon to Paul which would have been shown by his allowing Onesimus to remain in Rome. Paul is quite unwilling to keep Onesimus without the permission of his master, but he refrains from asking that Onesimus shall be sent back to Rome. Whatever service the slave renders the apostle must be under no compulsion from his master; it must not be even in response to a request from Paul. If Philemon is ever to grant the implied desire of Paul's heart for the return of Onesimus to Rome, it must be because Philemon himself desires it as a spontaneous act of love, not requested or even suggested by Paul.

Still another sentence is inserted before the apostle makes his long delayed petition: "For perhaps he was therefore parted from thee for a season, that thou shouldest have him for ever; no longer as a servant, but more than a servant, a brother beloved, specially to me, but how much rather to thee, both in the flesh and in the Lord."

It is in these words that Paul is describing the fault and flight of Onesimus. His master must have recalled the past with resentment. Before requesting that the past be forgiven, Paul places upon it this surprising, conciliatory, instructive interpretation. He intimates that it all may have been a part of God's loving plan. He does not affirm that it is so. He is modest in his interpretation of divine providences. "Perhaps" it was the case. As to the issue, however, there is no doubt. Of the underlying principle he is sure. It is this: God does bring good out of evil. He can use even the faults and failures of men to accomplish his purposes and blessing and grace. The disgrace and distress of Onesimus brought him to Rome, to Paul, and to Christ; now, as a transformed man he is returning to his master. The temporary separation has resulted in an eternal relationship: "He was therefore parted from thee for a season, that thou shouldest have him for ever." The brief loss of a slave is repaid by the permanent gain of a brother, and that, too, of a brother who is beloved by Paul and will be more dear to Philemon, both as a man and as a Christian.

At last Paul makes his definite request. It is that Onesimus shall be given a kind reception and complete pardon. In preparation for this request all the preceding sentences of the letter have been penned. Among the grounds for such a plea, the following have been advanced: The proposed action is just, or "befitting"; but "for love's sake" the request takes the place of what might have been a command. The petitioner is an aged Christian prisoner. He is under obligation to seek the welfare of one of his own converts. The changed character of the man justifies the request. Paul is sacrificing his own desire to his sense of duty to Philemon. He is leaving Philemon absolutely free to make his decision. He has implied that Philemon would willingly have allowed Onesimus to remain with Paul. He has intimated that the hand of God may be seen in the flight and return of the slave. Onesimus is returning not merely as a fugitive but actually as a beloved brother in Christ.

Enforced by such facts Paul makes his request: "If then thou countest me a partner, receive him as myself." Even in voicing this petition, so long delayed by graceful preliminary pleas, Paul appeals to a tender motive, namely, that of friendship. "If then thou countest me a partner" expresses no uncertainty. "Since you do so regard me" is what the words really mean. "Partner" denotes, however, more than a friend or a comrade. It denotes a relationship so close in its experiences as to involve mutual responsibilities. Because of their close fellowship in Christ, Paul requests Philemon to give Onesimus the same Christian welcome he would give to Paul himself.

There may linger in the mind of Philemon one reason for hesitation. Repentance should include restitution. The fugitive slave might show his sincerity by his willingness to surrender and to face any possible penalty; but how about the debt owed to his master? Paul anticipates such an objection by his memorable proposal: "But if he hath wronged thee at all, or oweth thee aught, put that to mine account; I Paul write it with mine own hand, I will repay it."

Evidently, then, the fault of Onesimus had included theft or the misuse of funds. Paul states the fact so delicately as to give no offense even to the guilty slave. He even states an alternative. Onesimus might have failed to return money advanced by Philemon. This may be the meaning of "oweth thee aught."

In any case Paul promises to repay all that Onesimus may owe. Whether Paul had private funds, or depended upon the gifts of friends to meet such special needs, is not certain. His promise, however, is definite. Possibly with a touch of humor, as he is addressing a close friend, he writes down his own name as signing a promissory note and obligating himself to pay the debt. It may indeed be regarded as a touch of pleasantry, for no one could seriously expect that Philemon would accept such a payment from the apostle even if Paul had the funds to give.

The improbability of such a transaction is made the more obvious by the phrase which follows: "That I say not unto thee that thou owest to me even thine own self besides." In reality, whatever Philemon might do for Onesimus at the request of Paul, Philemon would still be a debtor to Paul. He owed to Paul what money could never repay. He had received from Paul the knowledge of Christ. He owed to Paul his very soul. Of this fact, Paul indicates, he need not remind his friend, for it is certain to be in his mind and will impel Philemon to grant the request which the apostle has made, a request which Paul repeats under another form: "Yea, brother, let me have joy of thee in the Lord: refresh my heart in Christ."

The word "me" is emphatic. Philemon is in a position not only to benefit and relieve Onesimus but to give real delight to Paul to whom he is indebted for all that he holds most dear. He can rejoice the heart of his friend to whom he owes so much. At least to this extent he can repay what he owes. He can refresh and cheer and gladden the heart of Paul. Nor will it be a mere kindness of a friend to a friend. The transaction is "in Christ." It will please the Master and delight the Lord to whom both Paul and Philemon belong. Thus Paul finally describes the request, for which the whole epistle is written, as a plea for a kindness to himself; yet it is for himself as for one who has given his life wholly to the cause and service of Christ.

Paul closes his request by stating his absolute confidence that it will receive a favorable response: "Having confidence in thine obedience I write unto thee, knowing that thou wilt do even beyond what I say." The "obedience" of Philemon is not to a command. Paul has been careful not to claim authority. It is rather obedience to the call of Christian duty and of love voiced in the petition which Paul has made. What, however, does Paul expect "beyond" what he has asked? What more could be done besides receiving Onesimus as a Christian brother and canceling his debt? Some have conjectured that Paul wished to have the slave sent back to continue serving him at Rome; but Paul expects soon to leave Rome. Others have thought that Paul is requesting that Onesimus shall be set free; but this does not seem in accord with the words used by the apostle in stating his plea, v. 17. Probably the suggestion is of the kindness which may be shown to Onesimus in the future and even of his employment in spiritual work. At the least, Paul is expecting a ready and generous and cheerful granting of all that he has definitely asked.

He has, however, a further request: "But withal prepare me also a lodging: for I hope that through your prayers I shall be granted unto you." This brief additional request is not separated from the first. If Paul is soon to visit Philemon, this is an additional reason for immediately granting what has been asked in behalf of Onesimus. This "lodging" does not mean a place in Philemon's own house, but some place of entertainment which might be secured. The reply of Philemon to this delicate intimation would be naturally a cordial invitation that Paul should be his guest. Whether or not Paul ever visited Colossæ is not known. He is implying, however, that he believes

his friends are praying for him and that their prayers are
to be answered by his coming to them. If he does come,
it will be due to the goodness of God by whom Paul is
granted to them. For this visit to Colossæ he hopes. He
makes no definite promise, for he realizes that all prayer
must be offered in a spirit of submission to the will of God.
The expressed hope of such a visit forms a fitting conclusion to his request. It comes with the force of a gentle
compulsion; yet it is, after all, in keeping with the exquisite
delicacy with which the entire petition has been expressed.

It is not strange that this Epistle to Philemon is ap-
praised as a model of Christian courtesy nor that its specific request has been regarded as an illustration of a far
more marvelous intercession in which a divine Saviour is
heard to say, "If he hath wronged thee at all, or oweth
thee aught, put that to mine account."

4. THE CONCLUSION.   Philemon 23–25

**23 Epaphras, my fellow-prisoner in Christ Jesus, saluteth
thee; 24 *and so do* Mark, Aristarchus, Demas, Luke, my
fellow-workers.
25 The grace of our Lord Jesus Christ be with your spirit.
Amen.**

The letter closes with brief salutations from friends of
Paul who are with him in Rome, and with an apostolic
benediction.

The first of these salutations is from Epaphras, who of all
these persons mentioned would be best known to Philemon.
His full name was Epaphroditus; but he is to be distin-
guished from the messenger of that name who came from
Philippi to Rome bearing a gift to Paul. This Epaphras
was a native, or at least a citizen, of Colossæ. Through
his efforts and influence the church in Colossæ had been
established. This had been during the stay of Paul in
Ephesus. Years have passed and Paul is now a prisoner
in Rome. There Epaphras has visited him and is sharing
with him his confinement. This he is doing for the sake
of Christ and in the service of Christ. For this reason
the salutation is given in the following form: "Epaphras,

my fellow-prisoner in Christ Jesus, saluteth thee." The words, "Saluteth thee," mean in effect, "Wishes to be remembered to you." The word "thee," however, being in the singular number, indicates that the greeting is sent to Philemon alone and not to his family or to the congregation of Christians who met in his house. This is possibly because none but Philemon was known personally to the other companions of the apostle whose names are united here with that of Epaphras.

These are Mark, Aristarchus, Demas, and Luke. Two of them are among the immortals in the world of literature, for they are the authors of the Second and Third Gospels, which record the life and saving work of Christ. The Evangelist Mark is strikingly contrasted in social position and culture with the slave Onesimus; yet in personal experience they had something in common. Both failed in their early careers; both redeemed themselves, or were restored by the power of Christ; both became intimate associates of Paul and of great service to him.

Aristarchus was a trusted and devoted friend of the apostle, and his companion in travel, who like Epaphras seems to have shared willingly the tedium and distress of his imprisonment in Rome. Col. 4:10.

As to Demas nothing further is known save the one sad line written by Paul in the loneliness of his last imprisonment: "Demas forsook me, having loved this present world," II Tim. 4:10.

By way of contrast, in that same last letter of the apostle, the second letter written to Timothy, appears the phrase, "Only Luke is with me," thus surrounding the name of "the beloved physician" with a new halo of fidelity and glory.

All of these five are known as fellow prisoners or fellow workers of the apostle. The mere mention of their names gives to the epistle in which they appear the stamp of authenticity and of historic reality.

The apostolic benediction is in form and substance familiar to those who are acquainted with the writings of Paul. It is a prayer that the grace of Christ may be granted, not only to Philemon, but also to his household and to the group of believers who were wont to worship in his hospitable home. It intimates how the humblest acts of daily life can be transfigured with the very glory of heaven. It explains the secret of being able to write a purely personal letter, in reference to a fugitive slave, with such grace and courtesy and charm as to prove a model and an inspiration to the followers of Christ in every age and land. The secret is found by experiencing the blessing pronounced in the farewell words of the great apostle: "The grace of our Lord Jesus Christ be with your spirit. Amen."